The Urengoi Pipeline

Prospects for Soviet Leverage

John Van Oudenaren

This publication is supported by The Rand Corporation as part of its program of public service.

Library of Congress Cataloging in Publication Data

Van Oudenaren, John.
   The Urengoi pipeline.

   "R-3207-RC."
   Bibliography: p.
   1. Gas industry—Political aspects—Europe.
2. Urengoi Pipeline.   I. Title.   II. Rand Corporation.
HD9581.E82V36   1984   388.5   84-24868
ISBN 0-8330-0615-0

The Rand Publication Series: The Report is the principal publication documenting and transmitting Rand's major research findings and final research results. The Rand Note reports other outputs of sponsored research for general distribution. Publications of The Rand Corporation do not necessarily reflect the opinions or policies of the sponsors of Rand research.

Published by The Rand Corporation

R-3207-RC

The Urengoi Pipeline

Prospects for Soviet Leverage

John Van Oudenaren

December 1984

1700 MAIN STREET
P.O. BOX 2138
SANTA MONICA, CA 90406-2138

PREFACE

This report was prepared as a companion study to "Beyond the Pipeline: Soviet-West European Energy Trade and Its Implications for European Security in the Next Decade," by Thane Gustafson and Richard Nehring (forthcoming).

The report addresses the question of how the Urengoi natural-gas pipeline linking the Soviet Union and Western Europe could be used as an instrument of political leverage. It does not consider the technical aspects of energy supply in Europe, which are covered in detail in "Beyond the Pipeline." Instead, it concentrates on the reasons why the Soviet Union might use the pipeline to exert leverage and the economic, political, and psychological factors in Europe that would determine whether efforts to exert leverage would be successful.

The author would like to thank Henry S. Rowen, Keith Crane, and Edward Merrow for their comments on earlier drafts of this report, and Janet DeLand for her many helpful editorial suggestions.

SUMMARY

SOVIET ENERGY LEVERAGE

A country can be said to exercise economic leverage when it has the ability and the will to manipulate its own international (and, by implication, domestic) economic transactions in such a way as to compel or induce favorable political behavior in a target country.

The Soviet Union could use its energy-supply relationship with Western Europe as an instrument of leverage in two ways: (1) It could threaten or actually carry out a supply embargo, or (2) it could use energy to foster a gradual growth of West European dependence on the Soviet Union that would result in political influence.

The Soviet Union has tended to rely primarily on its role as a purchaser in trying to exercise leverage for political purposes. Nonetheless, it has on occasion exercised leverage as a supplier. In most cases, energy has been the commodity involved, and small Communist or third world countries the targets. The USSR has often used the provision of oil as a "carrot" and its cutoff as a "stick" to influence political behavior.

The emphasis in Soviet policy toward the major West European countries has been on positive, long-term "cooperation," with little hint of embargo or other forms of overt pressure. The Brezhnev regime sought to link the Soviet Union's growing energy export potential with its active détente policy by proposing expanded cooperation in energy matters and the convening of European energy conferences under the auspices of the Conference on Security and Cooperation in Europe (CSCE).

While the Soviet Union has shown no *fundamental* objection to the use of economic coercion against West European states, it has generally judged resort to such action not to be in its own long-term interests. An embargo of energy supplies would result in major economic costs to the USSR and would undermine Soviet efforts to create an "all-European" political order. An abortive Soviet gas cutoff that resulted in a loss of currency earnings, exclusion from large-scale cooperation projects, and a reconsolidation of the Western alliance could actually backfire and serve U.S. rather than Soviet interests.

There are scenarios, however, in which a Soviet energy cutoff is possible. The Soviet Union might resort to embargo in situations where it felt itself on the defensive and compelled to respond to a Western initiative. Developments that might provoke such a response could include a crisis in Eastern Europe involving real or perceived Western interference, "provocative" U.S. weapons deployments in Western Europe, or the creation of a multinational West European nuclear force. In situations that put it on the offensive, the Soviet Union would be less likely to threaten a cutoff of gas supplies and would probably rely on its local military superiority to create a regional *fait accompli,* while using the gas supply relationship to further an image of "businesslike" behavior during an international crisis.

WEST EUROPEAN RESPONSES

By 1990, West Germany, France, and Italy will import 30 to 40 percent of their gas supplies from the Soviet Union. Aware of the potential dangers of a gas cutoff, these countries are making emergency preparations that would enable them to withstand an embargo. European officials are confident that they could counter any Soviet embargo by drawing upon stores and reserve capacity and by switching to oil, a close substitute for natural gas for industrial uses.

In the late 1990s, the Soviet share of West European gas supplies could rise, and unless measures are taken now to diversify and further develop the intra-European emergency storage and transportation system, countering an embargo could become more difficult.

Attempts to counter a gas embargo might also lead to political problems. A crisis involving the pipeline would strain domestic consensus in the European countries as well as intra-European unity and solidarity with the United States. Diverging interests among the European countries and different attitudes toward the Soviet Union could hinder European Community (EC) or NATO-wide responses to an energy cutoff.

Perhaps more likely than an energy cutoff would be a gradual growth of European dependence on the USSR that could have political implications. With continued slow economic growth and high unemployment in Western Europe, the EC countries could turn increasingly to the East for markets. Western Europe might increase energy imports from the Soviet Union, which would enable the USSR to increase its imports of manufactured goods from the EC. Political factors, such as strains with the United States, could also encourage Western Europe to turn to the Soviet Union.

The probability of such developments exists but is not all that high. West European businessmen recognize that the Soviet market is not an answer to their economic problems. The Soviet import capacity is not likely to be sufficient to lock the large and diversified West European economies into dependent relationships. Nevertheless, the fact that these scenarios are at all plausible emphasizes Western Europe's probable long-term economic and political vulnerability and the need to give serious attention to possible Soviet attempts to exploit that vulnerability.

CONTENTS

I. INTRODUCTION

This report examines the implications for Western security of Soviet energy exports to Western Europe. It focuses on the largest and most controversial Soviet-West European energy venture, the recently completed Urengoi-Uzhgorod natural-gas pipeline. It also discusses other aspects of the energy trade between Western Europe and the Soviet Union.

The report has two parts. The first part considers energy as a potential instrument of leverage against Western Europe. It examines the Soviet record in using economic leverage and Soviet motives for promoting large-scale energy exports to the West, and it outlines several scenarios in which the Soviets might embargo exports or otherwise use energy as an instrument of political pressure.

The second part examines the European side of the relationship. It analyzes Western Europe's vulnerability and likely responses to two kinds of political pressure: (1) a sudden interruption of energy supplies aimed at forcing political concessions, and (2) a more gradual, long-term effort to encourage political accommodation through economic dependence.

While the report makes some attempt to deal with the technical aspects of the natural-gas trade in Europe, the main focus is on political and psychological factors. It is useful, up to a point, to measure West European vulnerability to physical shortages (in terms of levels of dependence, the ability to switch to alternative supplies, likely effects, and so forth), but in the final analysis, vulnerability can be understood only in a political context. Fundamentally, the question is how Western Europe, at a certain level of dependence, would respond politically to a crisis situation.

The historical record can offer clues, but no definitive answers to this question. In war and other extraordinary situations, many societies have shown an ability to endure extreme levels of privation. By the same token, the two oil shocks of the 1970s demonstrated that modest or even nonexistent shortages can lead to public outcries, economic disruptions, and abrupt changes in foreign policy. The emphasis in this report, then, is on the political setting in which Europe might have to respond to an actual crisis, as well as on those long-range factors which might create subtle forms of Soviet influence over West European policy in situations short of crisis.

II. SOVIET ENERGY LEVERAGE

DEFINING THE PROBLEM

A country can be said to exercise economic leverage when it has the ability and the will to manipulate its own international (and, by implication, domestic) economic transactions in such a way as to compel or induce favorable political behavior in a target country. A country can be said to be vulnerable to economic leverage when it lacks the ability or the will to counter an attempt at leverage by adjusting its own domestic and international economic behavior.

A deliberate interruption of supply by an exporter for political purposes would be an unambiguous exercise of leverage as it is defined in this context. Were the Soviets, for example, to cut off the flow of natural gas to a West European country in an attempt to compel that country's government to change its policies, they would be relying on their ability (political, legal, and physical) to implement the cutoff and their willingness to bear the economic costs (e.g., loss of hard-currency earnings and loss of reputation as a reliable supplier) of doing so. The success of such a leverage attempt would depend on the target country's ability to secure alternative sources of energy or incur economic losses (or some combination of the two) and its willingness to carry out compensating actions to counter the leverage attempt.

The use of leverage for political purposes is not necessarily limited to commodity exporters. At least in theory, West European governments could attempt to influence Soviet political behavior by ordering their companies to stop buying Soviet gas. When the United States announced that it would no longer import sugar from Cuba or, during the hostage crisis, oil from Iran, it was attempting to influence political behavior as a purchaser rather than a supplier.

Excluded from this definition are two kinds of power that are easily confused with economic leverage: market power, and political and military power that is used for economic *ends*. Market power is the influence that a country may exercise as a result of size and its share in the trade of a particular commodity. Saudi Arabia, for example, which accounts for a high percentage of world oil exports, is able to influence oil prices by virtue of its market share. Japan is a major purchaser of imported coal and can therefore influence the prices at which U.S. and Australian coal is traded. Influencing prices through the use of market power does not necessarily—indeed, does not usually—involve an attempt to reap political gains. Efforts to convert market power into political power (including the U.S. exercise of the grain embargo or the Arab countries' oil boycott of 1973–1974) in fact can lead to a loss of that market power without necessarily accomplishing the desired political result.

Firms and countries often find trade with countries that have market power economically advantageous—albeit less advantageous than it would be in the absence of that power. However, sovereign states are generally much more reluctant to conduct trade if doing so requires acceding to the political demands of a foreign power. In the 1970s, the Western countries accepted OPEC's market power and continued to import OPEC oil at higher prices than a free market might have dictated. However, most were unwilling to change their political behavior when Arab countries tried to use oil as a weapon for political purposes.

Although the exercise of market power is analytically distinct from the use of leverage for political purposes, in practice, a state attempting to exert political leverage by economic means must have at least latent market power for such an attempt to succeed. Countries with little or no ability to influence the prices at which goods are traded are even less likely to succeed in influencing the political behavior of other countries by interfering in a trading relationship. The Soviet Union generally accounts for too small a share of the world market in the commodities that it imports and exports to exercise market power. As an exporter of oil and gas, the USSR follows rather than establishes world price trends.

There is one exception to the general correlation between economic leverage and market power, namely, the granting of subsidies. States with little or no power to shift prices in their favor often have the option of shifting prices in a direction *unfavorable* to their own (economic) interests as a means of "buying" certain forms of political behavior. By granting subsidies, a state can lower the prices (to below-world-market levels) of the goods it exports or raise the prices (to above-world-market levels) of the goods it imports. When the Soviet Union sells oil to East European countries at below-world-market prices or buys Cuban sugar at above-market prices, it engages in this kind of behavior. Under the definition used here, such behavior is an exercise of economic leverage, even though it involves a net loss, in economic terms, for the country exerting the leverage.

The second type of power excluded by the definition is political and military power that is used for economic *ends*. Economic leverage results when a state manipulates economic relationships to bring about changes in political and security relationships, not when political and military power is used to change economic relations. When the Soviet Union used its political leverage over Finland to force that country to agree to conduct trade on a bilateral clearing basis, it was not exercising economic leverage as it is defined in this context. In contrast, when the Soviet Union ordered its import firms to stop purchasing oil from Iran because of Iran's crackdown on the Tudeh party, it *was* attempting to exercise economic leverage.[1]

In the controversy surrounding the Urengoi pipeline, almost no one argued that Western Europe was being compelled to buy gas from and sell pipe to the Soviet Union because of the latter's preponderant military and political power. Critics of the pipeline were in fact arguing the opposite, namely, that buying energy from and selling industrial products to the Soviet Union could lead to changes in prevailing political and security relationships by giving the Soviet Union opportunities to apply economic pressure.

Those who favored this argument cited two reasons why a mutually beneficial economic arrangement could give the Soviet Union leverage over West European political behavior. The first concerned the nature of the deal itself. West European governments were lending money to the Soviets to buy an asset that was located on Soviet territory and the functioning of which the Soviets would control. The second reason concerned the differences between the Soviet and the various Western political systems. The Soviets could cut off the gas trade and impose the costs associated with severing a beneficial economic arrangement on their people more easily than could the West European governments. How valid this argument was in practice remains a matter of dispute. In theory, however, the critics of the pipeline were correct in pointing out that for various reasons a mutually beneficial economic relationship can have harmful political consequences for one of the countries involved.[2]

The exertion of economic pressure—in the form of both punishment and reward—for political purposes has long been a feature of East-West trade. Few in Europe doubt that the sudden upsurge in Greek-Soviet trade and economic ties is attributable to the foreign policy of Prime Minister Papandreou. West Germany "buys" the political

---

[1]"Russia Cuts Out Iranian Oil," *The Guardian*, July 3, 1984.

[2]The energy glut of the early 1980s led critics of the pipeline project, in particular *The Wall Street Journal*, to argue that the project was not only politically dangerous but economically unsound as well. Whether this is in fact true can only be determined over the lifetime of the pipeline and of the Soviet-West European gas supply relationship. For a discussion of the economics of the pipeline, see Jonathan P. Stern, *International Gas Trade in Europe: The Policies of Exporting and Importing Countries*, Heinemann Educational Books, London, 1984, p. 152.

freedom of East Germans with hard currency and has granted credits to the East in the hope that doing so would smooth Eastern objections to U.S. missile deployments.[3] The United States under President Carter embargoed grain sales to the Soviet Union and cut back on Soviet fishing rights in U.S. waters to express displeasure at the invasion of Afghanistan.

As these examples indicate, the Soviet Union and some Western countries have tried to use economic threats and inducements to change the political behavior of other states. Unlike the United States, most of the West European countries do not believe in withholding trade with the East to compel changes in political behavior. However, the granting of economic rewards for political favors is also an act of leverage, if only because the failure to carry out these favors implies an economic opportunity cost for the target country. Under the definitions used in this study, East Germany is a target of West German leverage.

The Soviet and West European governments both exerted political pressures during the pipeline negotiations. However, most of the governments involved sought to influence the negotiations only to maximize their own economic benefits. The Soviets, for example, used their monopsonistic power to play suppliers and countries against each other in order to obtain the lowest prices and the most favorable credit terms for their imports of equipment. After 1981, when world energy markets turned unfavorable to the Soviet Union, West European governments used the negotiations about how much gas they would buy to try to compel the Soviets to step up purchases of manufactured and agricultural goods.[4]

As these examples suggest, state involvement in the pipeline project was confined to the exertion of pressure for economic purposes. But in the context of such massive, long-term projects, there is no guarantee

---

[3]Frederick Kempe and Roger Thurow, "Bonn Hastened Loan to East Germany to Mollify Soviets on NATO Missile Plan," *The Wall Street Journal*, August 19, 1983.

[4]In October 1982, after Agriculture Minister Edith Cresson failed to obtain an agreement with the USSR for the sale of 3 million tons of French grain, the French government directed domestic companies to stop buying Soviet oil (Robert Mauthner, "France Acts To Halt Soviet Oil Imports," *Financial Times*, October 28, 1982). In November 1983, Cresson (by then, the Minister for External Commerce) again protested the lack of Soviet orders for French equipment and was apparently rewarded with a major deal for Renault to modernize the Soviet automobile industry (David Housego, "Renault in Deal To Help Design and Produce New Soviet Car," *Financial Times*, November 28, 1983). The Italians, also concerned about trade deficits with the Soviet Union, exerted similar pressures, although from a position of greater strength, owing to their initial delay in concluding a gas purchase agreement. When the Italian government began negotiating an agreement in late 1983 to take gas from the pipeline, they demanded in return a promise of large Soviet orders of Italian goods (James Buxton, "Deficit with Moscow Worries Rome," *Financial Times*, December 19, 1983).

that political bargaining will remain simply a *means* by which states determine the price at which economic goods—gas on the one side, equipment and credits on the other—are traded. Political concessions could themselves become part of the price of certain deals. As economic relations become increasingly politicized and as publics and leaders become inured to the idea that economic and political ties go hand in hand, the possibilities for the exchange of political favors for economic gain and economic gain for political favors will no doubt increase. Thus far, however, the Soviet Union has not tried to use energy to induce or threaten the major West European states to change their defense and security policies.[5]

THE SOVIET RECORD

Despite its claims to the contrary, the Soviet Union has often attempted to use trade as an instrument of leverage. Soviet state trading organizations, acting under the direction of the party leadership, have tried to apply both supply- and demand-side leverage, in the former case by cutting off or threatening to cut off supplies for political purposes, in the latter by manipulating Soviet purchases of goods from other countries in attempts to encourage favorable political behavior.

Soviet attempts to use economic leverage, like those of the United States, have often been unsuccessful. As noted, the Soviet Union exercises relatively little market power over the goods it imports and exports. It also has to consider the economic costs of any political gains it might achieve through the use of leverage. In addition, many Soviet leverage attempts have been directed at other Communist countries, whose economic and political systems appear to be especially well-suited to rebuffing external pressures, whether exerted by the West or by a hostile Communist power.

The Soviet Union has used supply-side leverage in relatively few cases. During the depths of the cold war, it embargoed exports of chromium to the United States. In 1960, it cut off machinery and technology exports to China. It uses its control over access to fishing grounds in Soviet waters as an instrument of political pressure on Japan.[6] Apart from these and a few other scattered examples, energy has been the USSR's only supply-side lever. In numerous instances,

---

[5]In October 1984, Western observers were surprised when a Soviet trade unionist declared an embargo on the export of fuel (coal and oil) to Britain in support of striking coal miners ("Moscow Backs Miners with Halt on Coal Exports," *The Guardian*, October 31, 1984). Six days later, TASS denied that the Soviet Union had threatened an embargo.

[6]Eugene Moosa, "Japan Fishermen at Mercy of Soviets," *Los Angeles Times*, September 23, 1983.

the Soviet Union has used the provision of oil as a "carrot" and its cut-off as a "stick" to influence political behavior. In 1948, the USSR cut off oil exports to Yugoslavia in retaliation for Tito's deviation. In 1960, it did the same to China and Albania. After using the lure of cheap oil as an instrument to encourage Cuba's drift into the Soviet bloc, the Soviet Union suddenly cut back its oil deliveries in 1967 in an attempt to force Castro to accept greater Soviet influence on Cuban foreign policy.[7]

The Soviets have also used oil as a lever against non-Communist countries. In 1956, following the outbreak of war between Israel and Egypt, the Soviet oil-exporting firm informed the Israelis that its export licenses had been revoked by the Soviet government. In October 1968, after Ghana seized two Soviet trawlers suspected of transporting arms to rebel forces, the Soviet Union halted shipments of oil, despite the existence of a contract for the delivery of 700,000 tons of crude.[8]

The record of Soviet attempts at demand-side leverage, particularly in dealings with Western countries, is more extensive. The fact that Marxist-Leninist ideology stresses the struggle for markets among capitalists and the fact that few commodities, including oil, have been in short supply for long periods have encouraged Soviet leaders to regard the passive leverage derived from the purchase of Western products as more effective than the active leverage of a supply cutoff.

As far back as the 1930s, the Soviet Union used its purchasing power to pressure the United States to extend diplomatic recognition to the Bolshevik regime. Nikolai N. Krestinskii, Deputy Commissar for Foreign Affairs, wrote a report to the Politburo in which he stated:

> The maximum contraction and eventual full cessation of our purchases will be our most important and convincing instrument for putting pressure on America. The loss of Soviet markets, the importance of which has grown tremendously during the period of crisis, will more quickly impel American business and political circles to reconsider their traditional position of not recognizing the USSR.[9]

The Politburo evidently adopted Krestinskii's recommendations, since in 1932, U.S. exports to the Soviet Union dropped to $12.6 million from $103.7 million in the previous year.

---

[7]Carla Anne Robbins, *The Cuban Threat*, McGraw-Hill, New York, 1983, pp. 162–165.

[8]These incidents are described in Arthur Jay Klinghoffer, *The Soviet Union and International Oil Politics*, Columbia University Press, New York, 1977.

[9]*Dokumenty vneshnei politiki*, XIV, p. 527, quoted in John Lewis Gaddis, *Russia, the Soviet Union, and the United States*, John Wiley and Sons, New York, 1978, pp. 114–115.

Even in its energy dealings, the Soviet Union has generally promoted trade more because exports were the only way to earn the currency needed to import than because the export of energy in itself would result in political leverage. In the early 1950s, the Soviet Union capitalized on a fisheries dispute between Iceland and the United Kingdom by stepping in to become the main buyer of Iceland's fish, in the process becoming the main supplier of Iceland's oil. While the oil was useful as a method of payment, the real instrument of leverage was the purchase of fish and the resulting impact on Iceland's economy.[10]

As the Soviet Union has become a more active trading partner in Western Europe, the potential for using its purchasing power for political ends has increased. In the last several years, it has made numerous attempts at leverage. Although none of these attempts has been unambiguously successful, some may have had subtle effects on the thinking of West European leaders. When the Dutch refused a Soviet request in 1982 to allow the opening of a consulate in Rotterdam, an important transshipment point for Soviet grain, the Soviets diverted their grain trade to Antwerp and Hamburg.[11] While the Soviet Union denied any boycott of the Dutch port, Soviet grain imports through Rotterdam dropped from 1.4 million tons in 1982 to none in 1983.[12] It was also reported that if the demands for the consulate were not met, the Soviets would suspend talks with Philips, the Dutch electronics company, on plans to build a television manufacturing plant in the Soviet Union.[13] A similar incident is reported to have occurred in Belgium, following the expulsion of two Soviet nationals for espionage activities in the summer of 1982. According to a Brussels newspaper, the Soviets demanded that the expulsions be kept out of the press. Retaliatory actions if the demand was not met were to include cancellation of orders placed with the Belgian steel firm Sidmar, and, as in the Dutch case, a diversion of grain shipments from Antwerp.[14] There have also been frequent reports of Soviet threats to cancel contracts with Denmark for ships and other products unless the Danes broke ranks with

---

[10]Robert Loring Allen, *Soviet Economic Warfare*, Public Affairs Press, Washington, D.C., 1960.

[11]Walter Ellis, "Diplomatic Row Raises Fears in Rotterdam," *Financial Times*, February 10, 1983.

[12]Reuters dispatch, *Financial Times*, January 19, 1984.

[13]Walter Ellis, "Compromise over Facilities for Soviets in Rotterdam," *Financial Times*, January 19, 1983.

[14]*Le Soir*, January 22–23, 1983.

the European Community (EC) and lifted sanctions placed on the Soviet Union after the imposition of martial law in Poland.[15]

As these examples suggest, the Soviet Union has used supply cutoffs mainly against Communist countries and relatively weak third world countries, many of them already dependent on Soviet supplies or markets. The Soviet Union has used its purchasing power in dealing with all countries but has found, not surprisingly, that demand-side leverage is more effective on small countries with highly concentrated exports than on large countries with highly diversified economies. While the Soviets have shown no *fundamental* objection to exerting supply-side pressure on the major Western countries, in dealing with these countries they have downplayed hints of embargo and other forms of overt pressure and instead have emphasized positive, long-term "cooperation."

There are both economic and political reasons for this restrained posture toward the larger Western countries. Until the 1960s, the Soviet Union had difficulty securing outlets for its oil, as the U.S. government and the multinational oil companies sought to exclude it from world markets. In this period, the Soviet Union used exports of below-market-price oil and, after 1967, oil imports to weaken the influence of the major U.S. oil companies in the Middle East and Europe. For example, when the Western companies, in what was then still a buyer's market, refused to purchase oil from Iraq following Iraq's nationalization of Western property, the USSR stepped in to purchase the oil and then resold it (the USSR not being a net importer of oil) to Soviet customers in Asia.

In the late 1960s and early 1970s, as market power shifted from the buyers to the suppliers of energy, the Soviet Union was able to devote relatively less attention than previously to securing markets for its oil and natural gas. Although the changed world energy situation brought a new awareness to Soviet leaders of the West's potential energy vulnerability, the USSR was not quick to embrace energy as an instrument of leverage. Soviet policymakers no doubt remembered the earlier exclusion from world markets and were therefore cautious in evaluating the prospects for using energy to exert political pressure. Instead, they sought to reap major economic gains, especially in hard currency, and to establish a reputation as a reliable energy supplier. As the Soviet Union became a larger exporter of energy and used its hard-currency earnings to import grain and equipment from the West, its economic interest in maintaining trade also increased, somewhat offsetting the West's heightened vulnerability. This interest, while not

---

[15]John Palmer, "Danes Lift Soviet Sanctions," *The Guardian,* February 19, 1983.

an absolute guarantee against an energy embargo, militates against the use of the energy lever for political purposes.

The "offensive" element in Soviet energy export policy was confined for the most part to support for the Soviet Union's détente initiatives, as the Brezhnev regime sought to harness the energy export potential to its activist political strategy toward the West. At the 1971 Twenty-Fourth Party Congress, Premier Kosygin called for expanded cooperation in energy matters and the inclusion of all-European energy projects in the proposed Conference on Security and Cooperation in Europe (CSCE). A year later, at the Conference of European Institutes of International Relations, in Varna, Bulgaria, N. N. Inozemtsev, the head of IMEMO, outlined a "model" of the future which included a pan-European energy and transportation system.[16] In late 1975, several months after the conclusion of the CSCE in Helsinki, Soviet party leader Brezhnev called for the convening under CSCE auspices of all-European conferences on energy, transport, and environmental protection. In proposing these conferences, Brezhnev clearly wanted to underscore the physical (and, by implication, political) unity of the European continent and the contrasting isolation of the United States. With the same objective in mind, the Soviets proposed the interlinking of the European electricity distribution systems (which was opposed by the West European states) and the development of an inland water transportation system (supported by the West Europeans and now proceeding with the completion of the Rhine-Danube canal).

Taking advantage of the combined effects of the energy shortage and the developing political détente, in the 1970s the Soviet Union also launched a cautious attempt to establish itself as a middleman in the energy trade between the Middle East and Europe. In 1975, Soiuzgazeksport concluded a complex three-way deal with Iran and Ruhrgas of West Germany. Under the arrangement, Iran was to pipe gas to energy-deficient regions of the USSR near the Iranian border. This would make gas from northwest Russia available for export to Western Europe. The West Germans would pay for the gas by exporting large quantities of industrial goods directly to Iran. Iran withdrew from this project after the fall of the Shah, but the negotiations surrounding this three-way deal set the stage for the Urengoi project in the early 1980s.

In proposing the Urengoi pipeline, the Soviets were motivated primarily by economic concerns—the need to secure a future source of

---

[16]N. N. Inozemtsev, "Les Rélations Internationales en Europe dans les Années 1970," *Europe, 1980: The Future of Intra-European Relations,* reports presented at the Conference of Directors and Representatives of European Institutes of International Relations, Varna, Bulgaria, October, 1972, A. W. Sijthoff, Leiden, 1972, p. 130.

hard-currency earnings and the desire to channel Western capital and technology into the Soviet domestic energy program.[17] Political considerations were also a factor, however, as Soviet spokesmen themselves made clear. According to Genrikh Trofimenko, for example, Europe's "turning to Soviet gas" was a clear indication of Europe's attempt to "liberate itself from the octopus of U.S. policy." In the Soviet view, the pipeline was not intended to "serve purely selfish [i.e., Soviet economic] interests," but was also "a symbol for freeing Western Europe in one way or another from subordination to U.S. economic policy."[18]

As Trofimenko's remarks suggest, the Soviet Union's awareness of its potential ability to use energy—both its own export capacity and its middleman position in the energy trade—for political purposes clearly increased with the second oil crisis. However, it is noteworthy that even during the second oil shock following the fall of the Shah, the Soviets remained somewhat cautious about access to markets. Soviet leaders saw American exports of coal as a long-term threat to their own gas exports and to Poland's exports of coal to Western Europe, and were generally suspicious of U.S.-led efforts to limit their role in Western energy markets. Soviet policymakers believed, no doubt correctly, that energy leverage could be used most effectively not by threatening to cut off supplies, but by subtly hinting at Soviet strength and Western vulnerability, and working to foster long-term economic and political arrangements ostensibly designed to promote European security.

Ironically, the pursuit of these maximal political objectives probably provides Western Europe with added security against a gas cutoff, since the Soviet leadership would be reluctant to endanger fulfillment of them by imposing an embargo. This reluctance was strengthened by the heightening of concern in the Soviet Union about access to Western energy markets that accompanied the worldwide oil and natural-gas glut of the early 1980s. Despite the Soviets' politically "offensive" and commercially "defensive" motives for refraining from imposing an embargo, the possibility of such an action cannot be ruled out entirely. Under certain scenarios, the Soviets could resort to drastic measures of this kind. These scenarios are discussed below.

---

[17]Thane Gustafson, *The Soviet Gas Campaign*, The Rand Corporation, R-3036-AF, June 1983.

[18]Genrikh Trofimenko, interviewed in *Al-Watan* (Kuwait), October 30, 1982, in Foreign Broadcast Information Service, *Daily Report—Soviet Union*, November 4, 1982.

POSSIBLE SCENARIOS

The preceding examples of Soviet use of economic leverage all fall into either of two categories:

- Attempts, generally involving other instruments, to enhance Soviet political influence over other countries—to achieve, in short, a new *success* in Soviet foreign policy.
- Actions, following a Soviet foreign policy *failure*, that are designed either to salvage a deteriorating situation by heightened pressure or to "save face" by retaliation.

When the Soviet Union stepped in to take Iceland's fish in exchange for oil, it was hoping to increase its influence in that country.[19] When it cut off the supply of oil to Yugoslavia, it was reacting to a major setback. Both cases involved leverage, but of a different sort and for different reasons. This simple typology is useful in developing scenarios in which the Soviet Union might exert political pressure on Western Europe through the pipeline.

Based on what is known about past Soviet behavior, it seems likely that the Soviet Union would overtly use the leverage potential of the pipeline only in reacting to a policy failure, while it would rely on the latent leverage potential of West European economic dependence in its day-to-day pursuit of greater political influence over Western Europe. It would be most likely to use the "stick" of a supply cutoff in situations where it felt itself on the defensive and compelled to respond to a Western initiative. In situations where the Soviet Union was on the offensive, the Soviets would be less likely to overtly threaten a cutoff of gas supplies. Here, the USSR would probably rely on its local superiority to create a regional *fait accompli,* while using the gas supply relationship to further an image of "businesslike" behavior in a tense international situation. In both situations, the pipeline would tend to encourage inaction on the part of Western governments. At least in the local, West European context, it would exert a "conservative," system-preserving influence: It would help to forestall West European initiatives of which the Soviet Union disapproves and inhibit West European reactions to Soviet aggression in the Eastern bloc or the third world.

In its long-term policy toward Western Europe, the Soviet Union has worked to create an institutional structure and a body of quasi-

---

[19]Although there was no formal Soviet demand for political concessions, in 1954 Iceland watered down its bilateral security treaty with the United States. In addition, it was rumored that the Soviets successfully pressed for the inclusion of a Communist in the Icelandic government (Allen, *Soviet Economic Warfare,* pp. 41–42).

legal documents (such as the Helsinki Final Act) that lend substance to the claim that détente is an ongoing process leading to qualitative changes in the political order in Europe.[20] As was noted, Soviet pursuit of the long-term goal of promoting an all-European order and system of economic cooperation provides Western Europe with considerable security against a supply cutoff, since Soviet leaders would be reluctant to endanger these goals for a short-term political gain. However, it is necessary to consider whether a sharp and (from the Soviet perspective) unacceptable setback in this long-term policy might cause Soviet leaders to order an energy cutoff.

Although Soviet diplomacy displays great flexibility at the tactical level, it is hard not to see a certain "brittleness" or inflexibility in Soviet policy that arises out of the need to justify East-West relations in terms of a progressive theory of history and to square the "laws" of Marxism-Leninism with "bourgeois" international law. The Soviets claim, for example, that for ideological reasons Communist gains in Eastern Europe are "irreversible," and they have tried repeatedly to write this claim into agreements with Western states. While a distinction must be maintained between Soviet attitudes toward the "irreversibility" of Soviet gains in Eastern Europe and those toward trends outside the Communist world, Soviet behavior toward each region is affected by similar factors. The same vocabulary is used and the same general framework determines the analysis. Moreover, there are intermediate cases. Finland and Austria are non-Communist countries, but they are countries in which the USSR definitely asserts certain political and legal rights that it regards as fundamentally irreversible.

In the 1970s, the Soviets magnified the successes of their détente policy and overstated the degree to which they were able to "plan" the evolution of international relations. Conversely, they reacted vehemently to NATO's 1979 decision to deploy U.S. missiles, displaying what was probably genuine outrage at NATO's perceived attempt to reverse trends that Soviet leaders had come to consider all but irreversible. In the course of the missile controversy, the Soviets did in fact issue warnings that East-West ties, including trade, would suffer if new missiles were deployed. Although these threats eventually proved empty, it is conceivable that a future setback of this or even greater magnitude could cause a reaction.

---

[20]As an Italian delegate at the CSCE complained, "Détente was seen by the East not so much as a daily achievement of . . . good relations, but almost like a mechanical process, whose continuation (or irreversibility) was the precondition for the maintenance of good behavior internationally...." (Luigi Ferraris, *Testimonianze di un Negoziato,* CEDAM, Padua, 1977, pp. 302–303).

Despite Western insistence that the Helsinki Final Act was not a treaty under international law, Soviet and Eastern bloc governments have been quick to characterize Western actions of which they disapproved (e.g., the 1980 Olympic boycott and the economic sanctions against Poland and the Soviet Union) as not simply politically unacceptable, but in fact *illegal* under the provisions of the Act.[21] This attempt to endow a political document with legal status is to some extent a tactical device intended to give added weight to Soviet propaganda and diplomatic proposals directed at Western Europe, but it probably also reflects the Soviet tendency to see history in terms of a progression toward an outcome and to blur the distinction between "law" as a set of static norms and "law" as an expression of the inexorability of certain processes in nature and history.[22]

Because the Soviets blur distinctions between political and legal agreements, they could easily invoke the "legal" provisions of the Helsinki Final Act and various bilateral agreements to explain their refusal to meet obligations under existing contracts. It is worth noting the rationale that Poland, with support from the Soviet Union, has given for its failure to fulfill contractual obligations to Western lenders. Poland claims that U.S. sanctions are illegal, and it implies that U.S. illegality has negated any obligation on Poland's part to pay its debts. The Jaruzelski regime has demanded not only that the United States lift its sanctions, but that it pay Poland billions of dollars in compensation for its "illegal" acts. The Soviet Union has backed Poland in these claims. According to *Pravda,* U.S. sanctions

> contradict the basic principles and norms of international law. They are a serious violation of the provisions of the UN Charter, in particular, Article 1 Item 2, as well as the provisions contained in the Helsinki Conference Final Act, especially Principle I concerning sovereign equality and respect of the rights inherent to sovereignty, Principle VI on non-interference in internal affairs, and Principle IX concerning cooperation between states.[23]

It goes without saying, of course, that invoking these "legal" provisions would do little to protect the Soviet Union from the political and

---

[21]It is often pointed out in the West that the Helsinki Final Act "backfired" on the Soviets in that it stirred up dissidence in Eastern Europe. This was clearly an unintended result of the CSCE, however, and in no way vitiates the point about the link between the CSCE and the Soviet view of détente as process.

[22]Some scholars of Soviet law detect a failure to distinguish between law that is normative and static (*zakonnost'*) and law that is "scientific" (*zakonomernost'*). See John S. Reshetar, Jr., "The Search for Law in Soviet Legality," *Problems of Communism,* Vol. 28, No. 4 (1979), p. 64.

[23]*Pravda,* November 5, 1983.

economic consequences of an embargo, and Soviet leaders would have to weigh these consequences before taking action. The scenario outlined here virtually assumes a crisis in which the Soviet leaders would be prepared to act counter to certain of their political and economic interests in Europe—as these are currently perceived.

The pipeline could also be a factor in situations in which the Soviet Union took the initiative, probably outside Europe. While Soviet activism in the third world appears to have declined from its 1975–1979 peak, a new upsurge of activity in the Middle East, Africa, or Southwest Asia cannot be ruled out. Soviet initiatives might include intervention in post-Khomeini Iran, punitive expeditions into Pakistan against Afghan resistance fighters, support for separatist groups in Pakistan, and active intervention on the side of guerrilla movements in Southern Africa.

If the Soviet Union were to intervene militarily in the third world, one of its main objectives would be to forestall Western counter-intervention. Having done so, it would then launch diplomatic proposals (calls for regional conferences, mutual nonaggression pledges, talks with Soviet puppet regimes, and so forth) aimed at escaping political condemnation and obtaining international ratification of the *fait accompli*. Such, at any rate, was the pattern in the 1979 invasion of Afghanistan and the 1978 proxy invasion of Cambodia by Vietnam.

Under these circumstances, the Soviet Union probably would be strongly disinclined to order a gas embargo. Having created a favorable situation in the local setting, its main interest would be to "normalize" the situation by appearing as "businesslike" as possible and shifting the onus of escalation to the United States and others seeking a return to the status quo ante. While the Soviets would be reluctant to institute an embargo, they could derive advantages from hinting or even openly threatening that they were ready to take such action if Western Europe elected to cooperate with a U.S. sanctions policy. Theo Sommer, an influential editor of the German weekly *Die Zeit*, visited Moscow shortly after the invasion of Afghanistan and was warned about economic reprisals if the West Germans went along with U.S. sanctions. Sommer quoted a Soviet "functionary" as stating that "it is an open secret that you get not only natural gas from us, but also a considerable quantity of strategic raw materials. This has so far worked without any restriction."[24] Sommer was no doubt a useful if unwitting instrument for conveying an (unofficial) Soviet threat to the West Germans.

---

[24]Theo Sommer, "The Kremlin Does Not Believe in Words," *Die Zeit*, April 4, 1980, in Foreign Broadcast Information Service, *Daily Report: Western Europe*, April 4, 1980.

If Western Europe were to place sanctions on the Soviet Union following a future third world or East European crisis, in the Soviet view it would be interfering in a strictly internal or fraternal Communist matter. The Soviet Union could then resort to various "legal" arguments to embargo sales in response to such an "illegal" action. It could of course be argued that the Soviet Union would suffer further economic losses by undertaking such an action—as it no doubt would. It is important to keep in mind, however, that political factors would make Western Europe more vulnerable to the costs of a breakdown in trade than the Soviet Union. With opposition political parties possibly against sanctions in any case, the added leverage of the embargo threat could tip the scales of public opinion and government policy against such actions.

In a Middle East crisis, the pipeline could prove useful as a "carrot" to induce favorable West European behavior. In a tight world energy market, a crisis in the Middle East would certainly ignite fears of energy shortages on world markets, along with a rapid upward price spiral. Since gas pricing contracts are tied to a basket of oil-derived fuels, prices for Soviet natural gas would rise accordingly.[25] The Soviets could either profit economically from these rising prices or, alternatively, could offer to negotiate price reductions. Such reductions could be a sweetener to entice West European participation in one of the "conferences" or other diplomatic initiatives aimed at ratifying a *fait accompli* in the Middle East. If these initiatives took the form of the 1980 proposals, with three-way "guarantees" involving Western Europe, the Soviet Union, and the Middle Eastern producers, the Soviets could acquire expanded and mutually reinforcing leverage over both Europe and the Middle East, while shifting the burden of escalation to the United States. The effectiveness of Soviet incentives would of course depend heavily on world political and economic conditions, and in particular on world energy markets. In the 1984 situation of oil glut, in which Saudi Arabia has the capacity as a "swing" producer to dramatically increase its output at will, the Soviet ability to exploit energy insecurities for diplomatic gain is more limited than it was during 1979–1980, when energy shortages were feared, or than it is likely to be in the 1990s, when world energy markets are again expected to tighten.

The remainder of this report considers the factors that will influence how Western Europe would respond to short-term crises involving the pipeline as well as to more subtle attempts by the Soviet Union to exert influence through economic dependence.

---

[25]Prices for substitutable oil supplies would also rise in an emergency. This point is stressed by Jonathan B. Stein, "U.S. Controls and the Soviet Pipeline," *Washington Quarterly*, Vol. 5, No. 4 (1982), p. 55.

III. WEST EUROPEAN RESPONSES

THE CUTOFF SCENARIO

West European officials offer several arguments for their relative lack of concern about a Soviet gas embargo:[1]

1. The Soviet Union is a reliable supplier, with little or no record of manipulating energy sales for political purposes. In a crisis short of all-out war between East and West, the Soviet Union would be reluctant to endanger its main future source of hard currency by stopping gas sales. In a wartime situation, the gas no doubt would be cut off, but this would hardly matter in a situation whose outcome would be determined by military rather than political or economic factors.
2. Even if the Soviet Union were not a reliable supplier, neither are the OPEC states upon which Western Europe is already dependent. It is better to diversify among several potentially unreliable suppliers than to depend on one alone.
3. Western Europe's actual level of dependence on the Soviet Union will be small, and its ability to tap alternative sources of gas and to reallocate supplies within Europe will be great enough to ensure that a cutoff would be ineffective.

As the scenarios in Section II have shown, the premise of the first argument—Soviet reliability—is somewhat open to question. The Soviet Union has shown a willingness in extreme circumstances to use economic leverage in the pursuit of what its leaders see as overriding political goals, and therefore a gas cutoff cannot be ruled out altogether. But given the Soviet Union's economic interest in maintaining East-West trade and the role that trade plays in Soviet political strategy toward Western Europe, no Soviet leadership would undertake an embargo lightly.

---

[1]These arguments are developed in one form or another in Hans-Dietrich Genscher, "Toward an Overall Western Strategy for Peace, Freedom and Progress," *Foreign Affairs,* Vol. 61, No. 1 (1982), pp. 56–57; Klaus Matthies, "Soviet Natural Gas—A Threat to Western Europe's Security?" *Intereconomics,* September/October 1981; Jeremy Russell, "Import of Soviet Gas by Western Europe," *NATO's Fifteen Nations,* December 1982/January 1983; Roger Boyes, "Siberian Gas for Europe," *Europe,* No. 225 (1981); and John P. Schutte, "Pipeline Politics," *SAIS Review,* Summer 1982.

The second argument, based on the need for diversification, is also problematic. If Soviet and Middle Eastern supplies were embargoed simultaneously, diversification would be of little benefit. Fortunately for Western Europe, however, a simultaneous Arab and Soviet embargo is unlikely. The Arab countries themselves are much more reluctant than they have been in the past to suffer the economic and political costs of an energy cutoff. Even if the Arabs were to undertake such an action in the event of another Arab-Israeli war, the Soviet Union would not be likely to join with them in "solidarity." In 1973–1974, the Soviets praised the Arab embargo and the nationalization of Western oil companies, but they were unwilling to join in active support. In a future crisis, the Soviet Union would probably hesitate to endanger its economic and political relationship with Western Europe simply to give added support to Arab states that are already beholden to it.[2]

Soviet reliability and the possibility of simultaneous Soviet-Middle Eastern energy embargoes, while not unimportant, are clearly secondary to the issue raised in the third argument, namely Western Europe's ability to blunt the effects of a Soviet gas cutoff. If Western Europe is able to respond to an embargo with swift and efficient practical measures, it stands a good chance of being able to rebuff any Soviet attempt at leverage. Measures designed to cope with an embargo will of course also help to deter one (unless the Soviets are motivated purely by a desire to "save face" or to retaliate—a possibility not to be dismissed in light of Soviet behavior toward Yugoslavia and China). Given the centrality of this argument, then, the following discussion of supply cutoff focuses on dependence and vulnerability.

Western Europe's ability to cope with an energy crisis has improved dramatically since 1973–1974. The EC managed to reduce the share of imported oil in its overall energy requirements from about 59 percent in 1973 to 47 percent in 1983, partly by increasing the share of natural gas in Community energy requirements.[3] At the same time, the world oil market itself has improved for buyers, with the addition of major producers such as Mexico and the United Kingdom reducing the relative importance of the volatile Persian Gulf. The partial diversification from oil to natural gas has improved Western Europe's energy security,

---

[2]This relatively optimistic picture of course leaves aside the prospect of a Soviet military advance against the Persian Gulf and its supplies of oil. Such a possibility, although a serious one for the Atlantic Alliance, will not be explored in this report, which is concerned with peacetime economic leverage rather than with the Soviet military threat to Western interests.

[3]Commission of the European Communities, *The Energy Situation in the Community, 1983,* Brussels, 1984.

without, in the view of EC officials, creating new vulnerabilities of its own.

During the negotiations for the pipeline deal, the West German government declared a maximum allowable level of 30 percent dependence on Soviet sources for natural gas, later amending this to 40 percent of consumption when the growth of gas demand in West Germany slowed.[4] The other West European countries have generally followed the German lead in designating 30 to 40 percent of consumption as a politically safe upper limit. National and EC officials are confident that, barring a major upheaval in the Middle East, these projected import levels will not result in a potential for Soviet leverage.

The current energy situation in Western Europe tends to support this optimistic view. The overall situation is one of gas surplus, in which the Soviets are unable to find buyers for even the volume of gas they had originally hoped to sell. Ruhrgas turned down Soviet offers to begin deliveries through the new pipeline ahead of schedule.[5] Gaz de France is attempting to renegotiate its contracts in order to hold down the level of its initial purchases.[6] Having contracted for additional supplies of gas from Algeria, the Italians delayed conclusion of a gas agreement for more than two years after declaring a "pause" in negotiations in January 1982 in response to the imposition of martial law in Poland. When they finally signed a contract with the Soviets in May 1984, it was for the purchase of only about half the gas Soiuzgazeksport originally had hoped to sell.[7] In this situation of relative energy abundance, it would be pointless for the Soviets even to hint at a gas embargo.

Against the background of this improved situation, however, are a number of potential problems. First, conditions are not likely to remain favorable for oil and gas importers indefinitely, and European planners recognize that they must view energy vulnerability with reference to the less favorable energy situation that is expected to develop after 1990. Second, while the partial diversification from oil to natural gas has been useful in lowering Western Europe's dependence on

---

[4]Boyes, "Siberian Gas for Europe," p. 29.

[5]Ruhrgas agreed to take the first deliveries in late 1984, as set forth in the original contract (John Davies, "West Germany: Energy," *Financial Times,* October 31, 1983). In September 1984, it successfully negotiated a reduction in the gas price with Soiuzgazeksport (James Bell, "Ruhrgas Settles Price for Supplies of Siberian Gas," *Financial Times,* September 4, 1984).

[6]"French Gas Utility Seeks To Cut Soviet Imports," *Journal of Commerce,* May 4, 1984.

[7]Alan Friedman, "Italy Signs 24-Year Siberian Gas Contract," *Financial Times,* May 18, 1984.

OPEC and Arab producers, it has created new problems that arise from the way gas is traded and transported.

Because of the fungibility of oil as a commodity and the flexibility of world oil markets, the 1973–1974 oil crisis did not require forceful action on the part of the West European governments. Many of the measures that helped to blunt the effects of the oil embargo were undertaken by the multinational oil companies, which were able to serve as political buffers between producing and consuming countries and reallocate world oil supplies in ways that negated the effects of the embargo. Much of this flexibility has been lost with the tying of gas to a specific transportation path that can be interrupted by the producing country. To cope with a possible supply cutoff under these circumstances, the West European countries will not only have to undertake technical measures that will allow them to replace embargoed gas, but they will also have to work out political arrangements for invoking these measures in the event that doing so becomes necessary.

Technical Measures

The EC Commission estimates that in 1990, imports of gas from the Soviet Union will represent 19 percent of total EC gas supplies and 4.5 percent of total energy supplies, with the three major importers—West Germany, France, and Italy—all 30 to 40 percent dependent on Soviet sources (see Table 1).[8] These import levels will be low enough to allow for switching to alternative sources of fuel and drawing upon excess gas capacity in the event of a Soviet cutoff. For most industrial uses, including the generation of electricity, fuel oil is a close substitute for natural gas. As long as oil supplies remain adequate, switching to bivalent burners can provide security against a gas cutoff even at very high levels of imports.[9] For other uses, such as home heating, in which it is not possible to switch from gas to oil in an emergency, nonsubstitutable gas usage can be maintained by drawing upon stores and increasing domestic production. European Community officials are confident that for the remainder of the decade, spare production capacity within the EC, especially in the Netherlands, will be adequate to make up for shortfalls resulting from any Soviet cutoff. They also report that the existing pipeline network is large and flexible enough to move supplies to embargoed regions.

---

[8]Data derived from Commission of the European Communities, *Communication from the Commission to the Council Concerning Natural Gas,* Brussels, 1984.

[9]Stein, "Natural Gas and International Trade," p. 51.

Table 1

NATURAL GAS SUPPLIES IN 1982 AND 1990

Country	Total Gas Consumption (mtoe)		Total Gas Imports		Imports from the USSR		Soviet Gas Share of Total Gas Consumption (%)		Soviet Gas Share of Total Energy Consumption (%)	
	1982	1990	1982	1990	1982	1990	1982	1990	1982	1990
FRG	38.4	52.9	27.6	39.4	7.9	15.7	20.6	29.7	3.2	5.3
France	21.2	26.3	15.1	24.0	3.1	9.4	14.6	35.7	1.75	4.5
Italy	22.0	32.9	11.1	24.3	7.0	11.8	31.8	35.9	5.3	6.6

For the late 1990s and beyond, there is greater cause for concern, as expected declines in domestic gas production, continued increases in demand, and a tightened international oil market should strengthen the Soviet Union's leverage potential. European Community imports of natural gas from all sources are expected to increase from 28 percent in 1982, to 43 percent in 1990, to between 50 and 60 percent in 2000. A key issue is which countries will supply the more than half of Europe's gas that will have to be imported in the late 1990s. Contracts for these additional supplies have not yet been signed, but West European flexibility in choosing new sources will be constrained by the investment decisions made in the next several years.

The EC has identified six potential extra-Community sources: the Norwegian Troll field, Algeria, liquefied natural gas (LNG) from Nigeria, LNG from Cameroon and the Ivory Coast, distant countries such as Canada and the Persian Gulf states, and the Soviet Union. Of these six sources, only Algeria and the Soviet Union are well positioned to increase substantially the volume of their exports to Western Europe without making major new investments. Unless the West European countries are willing to make politically motivated (but possibly economically noncompetitive) investments in Norwegian and sub-Saharan African projects, Soviet gas imports could rise to well over 40 percent of total consumption.

With higher imports, the requirements for intra-EC storage and surge capacity and for emergency transportation also will increase after 1990. The EC countries are committed to developing an intra-Community gas grid, but there is some controversy over how much progress is actually being made along these lines. Some experts argue that although the West European pipeline grid will be interlocked in a way that permits supply switching, it could be quickly overloaded if the volume of gas flowing through the East-West lines from Siberia had to be replaced from North Sea and Dutch supplies that could move only through the North-South network.[10] The EC Commission itself concludes that while provisions for the remainder of this decade are adequate, the Community should be concerned about transportation and storage capacity for the 1990s.

The willingness of West European governments to invest in diversification and backup systems will be influenced by numerous economic and political factors. A major determinant will be the world price of energy, which most forecasters predict will fall or remain steady for the rest of the decade.[11] Falling prices are already having an effect on efforts to develop domestic resources and diversify imports. Most of the energy projects that have been canceled to date involve coal, which has proven uneconomical and ecologically objectionable to West European publics.[12] Natural gas prices are also turning downward, however, making development of expensive Norwegian and African gas fields increasingly difficult to justify on economic grounds.

While access to Soviet gas was originally sought in the interests of diversification of supply, it has now become at least a temporary impediment to diversification itself. Some observers even see the potential for a Soviet gas "dump" on the European market,[13] the threat of which will cast a cloud over investment in other projects. (This turn of events was not entirely unforeseen. In early 1982, the *Petroleum Economist* observed that "European initiatives for the development of overseas resources may to some extent be stifled by the arrangement of very large long-term supplies from the USSR, and . . . the new Soiuzgasexport contracts may therefore have a less favorable effect on Europe's long-term supply prospects than would appear at first sight."[14]) Arguing that NATO countries should be willing to pay a premium to develop a politically secure source of energy, the Norwegian government has asked for U.S. assistance in encouraging

---

[10]Wilfried Prewo, "The Pipeline: White Elephant or Trojan Horse?" *The Wall Street Journal*, September 28, 1982.

[11]"World Economic Outlook," *Econoscope*, Royal Bank of Canada, January 1984.

[12]David Fleming, "Coal-Conversion Plans Suffer Setback in Italy," *Journal of Commerce*, November 28, 1983; John Tagliabue, "Cutback in German Coal Near," *The New York Times*, September 27, 1983.

[13]Ian Hargreaves, "W. Europe Faces Possibility of Gas Glut," *Financial Times*, January 4, 1984; see also Véronique Maurus, "Le Marché du Gas Bloqué," *Le Monde*, August 7, 1984.

[14]B. A. Rahmer, "Soviet Union: Big Gas Deal with West Europe," *Petroleum Economist*, Vol. 49, No. 1 (1982); and Richard Bailey, "Impact of the Euro-Soviet Gas Pipeline," *National Westminster Bank Quarterly Review*, August 1982, p. 20.

Britain and the continental countries to agree to buy expensive gas from the North Sea rather than Soviet gas at lower prices.[15] However, even British Gas is now considering imports of gas from the Soviet Union through a cross-channel pipeline to France or the Netherlands.[16]

As the behavior of British Gas suggests, paying a premium for energy security is easier for governments to support in principle than to carry out in practice. The West European governments are all strongly committed to fighting inflation and will be wary of programs that either lead to higher energy costs or require direct government subsidies. The West European countries are highly export-conscious and will be concerned about the effects of higher energy prices on competitiveness in world markets. Indeed, the plans to construct the Urengoi pipeline itself took shape during and just after a period in which European governments were complaining about the advantages U.S. companies, particularly in the textile and chemical industries, were enjoying as a result of price controls that kept U.S. energy costs below world-market levels. The pipeline was believed, at least initially, to be a low-cost source of energy for European industry and hence a factor that would contribute to Europe's competitive position in home and third markets. The advantages enjoyed by U.S. producers in the late 1970s, it should be noted, will be modest compared to those that Saudi Arabia and other Middle Eastern countries will enjoy when petrochemical plants now under construction become operational.[17]

European governments and businessmen are also likely to be sensitive to possible linkages between future purchases of energy and export opportunities for European businesses. By offering to step up purchases of industrial goods from West European countries, the Soviets may be able to induce these countries to take higher volumes of gas. According to East European sources, Italy and the Soviet Union signed a protocol in May 1984 which committed the USSR to diminish its trade surplus with Italy and to direct its purchases to small and medium-sized enterprises. The USSR agreed to spend 3.5 trillion lire (some $2 billion) on Italian goods each year, an amount roughly equivalent to Soviet gas sales to ENI, the Italian energy company.[18]

---

[15]Jan Tystad, "US Intervenes in North Sea Gas Deal," *The Guardian,* March 15, 1984.

[16]Dominic Lawson, "Britain Considers Purchase of Gas from Soviet Union," *Financial Times,* October 12, 1984.

[17]The search for cheaper feedstocks is leading European companies to team up with the Soviets to respond to the commercial threat from the Arab states ("ICI in Talks on £150m Plant for Russia," *The Guardian,* February 6, 1984).

[18]"Link Between Soviet Purchases in Italy and Gas Supply," *East-West,* July 3, 1984.

This tying of gas purchases to industrial exports can of course work against the Soviets as well. The Dutch government decided not to purchase any Urengoi gas when the Soviets failed to place orders for pipe or industrial equipment with firms in the Netherlands.[19] In 1982, the French agreed to pay a "political" price for Algerian gas in exchange for greater Algerian purchases of French products—in effect, they chose to favor a third world supplier at the expense of the Soviet Union. However, the deal with Algeria proved to be extremely expensive and France has negotiated an agreement that will scale back the volume of imports, thereby making the Soviet Union its largest gas supplier.[20] Although it is too early to tell, the Soviet Union's ability to offer gas at low prices, along with its willingness to tie sales of gas to stepped-up purchases of industrial and agricultural goods, could prove a combination that West European political leaders may find difficult to resist, and may push up levels of dependence on Soviet gas in the 1990s.

Political Factors

Even if the West European governments overcome the various economic and political obstacles and make the investments that will enable them to replace Soviet gas in a crisis, they still will face the additional problem of working out political arrangements among themselves for responding to Soviet pressures in an emergency. The EC Commission acknowledges that "in a fully interconnected Community market, which is not the case today, it would be sufficient if adequate diversification existed at the Community level, provided always that Member States were prepared in future—as they have already agreed to do in respect of oil—to assist each other in case of supply disruption."[21]

Unfortunately for planners, it is extremely difficult to predict the political circumstances that would surround a Soviet gas embargo. Although in any discussion of the political requirements for responding to such an embargo the 1973–1974 oil embargo and Western Europe's response to it loom large, there are likely to be major differences between those events and a future Soviet embargo.[22] Whereas the Arab

---

[19]David Brand, "Europeans Subsidized Soviet Pipeline Work Mainly to Save Jobs," *The Wall Street Journal*, November 2, 1982.

[20]Paul Betts, "Algeria Agrees To Slow Gas Exports to France," *Financial Times*, September 20, 1984.

[21]*Communication from the Commission to the Council Concerning Natural Gas*, p. 11.

[22]On October 17, 1973, the Organization of Arab Petroleum Exporting Countries (OAPEC) announced its intention to enforce successive monthly cuts in oil production until Arab political demands were met. Importing countries were divided into three categories: (1) unfriendly countries—the United States and the Netherlands—which

oil embargo was unambiguous in political intent but rather inefficient in preventing supplies from reaching target countries, a gas cutoff could have the opposite characteristics: It could be ambiguous in terms of political intent but totally effective in stopping the flow of gas from the supplier to the importing country. Soviet authorities could stop the flow of gas for what they might call "technical reasons" but leave considerable ambiguity as to whether a real attempt was being made to extract political concessions.[23] If the level of dependence were sufficiently high, these "technical" disruptions could have severe economic consequences. The Soviets could incur significant costs, commercially and politically, by engaging in a "covert" embargo, but these costs might be less than the costs of openly abrogating supply agreements.

The fact that the Soviet Union, unlike the Arab states, threatens Western Europe with military power also cannot be overlooked. Even if Western Europe had the means to physically replace embargoed supplies, a cutoff of Soviet gas would raise concerns in Europe that went beyond simple fear of energy shortages. In a severe East-West crisis, it is difficult to say whether the Soviet Union would derive any *additional* leverage from the pipeline beyond that exerted by its military forces in the face of imminent war. In war or a prewar crisis, the role of the pipeline would become secondary, much the way it would in the case of a Soviet military attack on the Persian Gulf. It is worth noting, however, that in a crisis situation, the Soviets might be able to use a gas cutoff to show Soviet "resolve" and to signal the seriousness of Soviet *military* intentions. While in "normal" circumstances the costs of an energy cutoff work in Western Europe's favor and encourage stability in East-West relations, in a crisis evidence of Soviet willingness to endure costs might be intimidating rather than reassuring.

Any uncertainty on the West European side over whether an interruption of supply was "technical" or "political," or whether the embargo was a possible prelude to military action, would exacerbate the political problems governments would face in responding to an embargo. All of the difficulties inherent in planning for a "peace-to-

---

were to receive no oil; (2) "friendly" countries, including Britain and France, which were to receive their normal allotments of oil; and (3) all other countries, which would face phased reductions of 5 percent per month (see Robert J. Lieber, *Oil and the Middle East War: Europe and the Energy Crisis,* Harvard Center for International Affairs, 1976, pp. 12–13; and Romano Prodi and Alberto Clo, "Europe," *Daedalus,* Vol. 104, No. 4 (1975)).

[23]In the winter of 1981–1982, several European countries experienced interruptions in Soviet gas deliveries that were deliberate but were ascribed by the Soviet authorities to "technical difficulties." These interruptions did not involve attempts to exert political pressure, however; they were caused by difficulties in the Soviet energy system and problems in supplying Eastern Europe.

crisis" transition would be encountered in the area of energy supply as well. Just as the capability to rapidly reinforce Western Europe in the event of a military crisis is only as good as the willingness of political leaders to use that capability, measures to meet an energy crisis are only of value if they are actually used in a timely fashion by political leaders. In both the military and the energy supply cases, decisive action is required precisely when it is likely to be seen or characterized as "provocative" and destructive of efforts to defuse the situation by political means.

In view of the political difficulties West European governments would face in countering a Soviet gas embargo, even countries with the technical ability to respond to one might prefer some form of face-saving accommodation with the Soviet Union. The Soviets could make accommodation easier by not making explicit political demands—a tactic they have used in the past, for example, in diverting their grain trade from Rotterdam. For their part, West European governments could simply deny having yielded to pressure or having made concessions. In 1974, when France acceded to Arab requests to work against creation of the International Energy Agency (IEA), it did not admit that it had yielded to pressure but instead attacked the threat of "American domination."[24] Particularly in the case of crises in third areas in which the Soviets were backing a side whose claims appeared to have some legitimacy (e.g., the Arab states against Israel or a national liberation movement in a future crisis in Southern Africa), a West European state could align with the Soviet Union and claim that it had done so not in response to pressure, but because of its reading of the dispute itself.

Even if these initial difficulties were overcome and the West European governments decided to invoke the technical measures needed to meet a Soviet embargo, they might still have difficulty in forging the unified response that would be necessary for these measures to succeed. A crisis involving the pipeline could strain domestic consensus within the individual West European countries, intragovernmental unity in Western Europe, and solidarity in the Atlantic Alliance.

It is probably less useful to try to identify domestic groups that might pose problems in an embargo—an exercise that is bound to be highly speculative—than to ask who might have an interest in opposing resistance to a Soviet embargo. Three groups must be considered:

- Those who support the objectives of the Soviet Union (Communists and fellow-travelers).

---

[24]Lieber, *Oil and the Middle East War*, p. 20.

- Those who do not support Soviet objectives but would rather compromise with Soviet demands than endure economic sacrifice.
- Those who neither support Soviet objectives nor fear economic loss but are concerned about the maintenance of peace and therefore would be willing to compromise with Soviet demands.

The strength of the first of these groups in the various countries is well known and need not be discussed in this context. In divisive domestic debates, the Communists can play a major role in raising and defining issues for the public. The obvious example is the "neutron bomb" debate in the Netherlands, which owed much to the work of the Dutch Communist party. On the organizational level, the Communists can multiply their strength by forming alliances with other groups—the economically affected and those concerned about peace—that are likely to resist a firm stance against Soviet pressure.

Those affected economically by a gas cutoff would include consumers, bankers, and exporters. As noted, West European governments are instituting emergency measures to blunt the potential effects of a total gas embargo. Under these measures, industrial users of gas would switch bivalent burners to oil, leaving available supplies of gas for home heating. Consumers would therefore not be heavily affected. It is unlikely, however, that countries could lose over 30 percent—and some regions, such as Bavaria, might lose as much as 90 percent—of total gas supplies without some temporary dislocation. A period of days or weeks could pass before all redistribution problems are worked out. Temporary heat shortages, layoffs, and administrative difficulties would embarrass governments and intensify pressure for a political settlement that would restore the flow of gas.

An embargo could also affect bankers and exporters. These effects would be indirect but more severe than those on consumers. In discussions of the pipeline and its security implications, West European governments have generally argued that because the Soviet Union needs a continuing stream of credits and technology, bankers and exporters are guarantors against rather than potential victims of a Soviet embargo. This observation no doubt applies under "normal," noncrisis circumstances. However, in a crisis severe enough to occasion a major reevaluation of Soviet policy toward Europe, different standards would apply. A breakdown in the Soviet-West European energy relationship in effect would set in motion an economic war of attrition. The Soviet Union would suffer losses in such a "war," but a rational Soviet leadership could conclude that the Soviet Union is economically and politically better prepared to cope with these losses than are the West European countries. The Soviets might calculate that Soviet losses (i.e., the effects of a hard-currency shortage) could be diffused throughout the population (e.g., a loss of hard currency would mean less meat and milk for everyone), while in the West, the brunt of the economic losses would fall upon particular groups. These groups could be expected to lobby vigorously for concessions that would induce the Soviet Union to lift or refrain from imposing its embargo.

Were the Soviets to lose their hard-currency earnings in a gas cut-off, they might default on their loans even before cutting back on imports.[25] Such a default would be all the more likely if the Soviets had managed to shift the legal responsibility for the cutoff to the West Europeans.[26] Exporters also would suffer from a breakdown in trade and could be expected to press for an accommodation resulting in its restoration. When the Soviet Union hinted that it would continue to divert trade from the port of Rotterdam if the demand for a Soviet consulate was not met, the mayor of that city warned that jobs were at stake and urged the Dutch government to seek a compromise. When the government of India cut purchases of machinery from the Soviet Union in order to buy more advanced Western products, the Soviets retaliated by drastically cutting imports of Indian goods. Indian manufacturers successfully lobbied the government in New Delhi to restore purchases of Soviet goods and thereby preserve their own trade.[27] The Dutch and Indian cases are different, in that in the former the USSR tried to use economic leverage to secure a political gain, whereas in the latter it sought to protect its economic interests (although the Soviet Union does see its political influence in India threatened by a decline in trade). However, both cases illustrate the behavior of private exporters when faced with cutbacks—either politically or economically motivated—of sales to the USSR.

Domestic political problems would be further exacerbated if the causes of the crisis were obscure or ambiguous. With the breakdown of the foreign-policy consensus in major West European countries, the distinction between initiation of and response to action has become

---

[25]It is interesting to note that the Algerian government, locked in a dispute with companies in Spain and the United States over the cancellation (for commercial reasons) of gas import contracts, has tried to exert pressure through banks carrying loans to Algeria. See Francis Ghiles, "Algeria Lobbies U.S. Banks over Suspended Gas Deal," *Financial Times*, March 26, 1984.

[26]The credibility of the default threat depends on the net debt position of the Soviet Union. According to the Bank for International Settlements, the Soviet Union in 1983 had a gross debt of $28.8 billion, which was partially offset by some $11.2 billion of assets in Western banks (Peter Norman, "USSR's Debt Is Much Bigger than Believed," *The Wall Street Journal*, May 3, 1984.

[27]John Elliot, "Big Democracy, Smaller Significance," *Financial Times*, March 22, 1984.

increasingly blurred. When the Soviet Union invaded Afghanistan in late 1979, many in Western Europe argued that following the U.S. failure to ratify SALT and the December 1979 NATO two-track decision, the USSR "had nothing to lose" by abandoning its earlier restraint. In the course of the emotional debate surrounding the U.S. missile deployments, publications such as *Stern* and *Der Spiegel* sought to prove that the deployments had been planned as far back as the early 1970s and that the Eurostrategic imbalance to which Helmut Schmidt pointed in 1977 was only an excuse.[28] Following the Soviet downing of Korean Airlines Flight 007 in September 1983, there was a surprisingly strong disposition in Europe to accept the Soviet view that this action was a response—albeit an inappropriate one—to a U.S. provocation.[29] In a situation in which West European public opinion was sharply divided over who "started" the crisis, the Soviets could put forward demands that it claimed were simply a "response" to a Western provocation. Even if only vocal minorities were disposed to accept the Soviet claim, government efforts to forge a forceful response to Soviet demands would be undercut.

If the prospects for domestic consensus in a crisis are not good, the outlook for unity among governments within the EC and NATO is also uncertain. The 1973–1974 Arab oil embargo was a major test for the EC—one that it failed to meet, in the view of most observers.[30] The Community was unable to devise a formula for sharing available supplies of oil and unable to adopt a political position on the Middle East that would support the Dutch without endangering the privileged position of France and Britain.

European officials argue that divide-and-conquer tactics, which they admit were used with some success by the Arabs, could not work in the case of a gas cutoff, since the very nature of the pipeline, which physically links the importing states, will force unity upon them whether they like it or not.[31] To embargo France, the Soviet Union would also have to cut off gas to West Germany (to prohibit sharing), while it

---

[28]See the series by Wilhelm Bittorf, "Schiessplatz der Supermaechte," *Der Spiegel,* Nos. 28–31, 1981.

[29]See, for example, the editorial by Rudolf Augstein (publisher of *Der Spiegel*), "Moral, Moral, Moral," *Der Spiegel,* No. 37 (1983); and Jon Nordheimer, "Mrs. Thatcher Criticizes Europe on Flight 007," *The New York Times,* September 19, 1983.

[30]See Lieber, *Oil and the Middle East War,* pp. 44–52.

[31]Strictly speaking, this argument is only partially true. The point at which the gas pipelines to Western Europe divide into northern and southern branches—the former running into West Germany, the latter to Austria and Italy—is in Czechoslovakia. The Soviets thus retain some ability to selectively embargo different regions of Europe.

would be unable to embargo West Germany without also cutting off supplies to France.

This argument has some merit, but only as it relates to the physical means of distribution. It neglects the political aspects of an embargo. In a pipeline cutoff directed at West Germany but not at France, the Germans would not be likely to simply seize the gas, but would probably try to work out an arrangement with France for sharing. In some circumstances, the French might choose not to cooperate in such an arrangement (not being members of the IEA, the French are not committed in advance to sharing available oil supplies). If, as is more likely, they did try to share with the Germans, the Soviets could declare that such action would be cause for cutting off sales to France as well. A difficult political situation might then arise, leading the French and perhaps the Germans themselves to conclude that some exports of Soviet gas to Europe were better than none, and to refuse to provoke the USSR into a total cutoff.

If the Soviets ordered a total gas embargo, states such as Norway and the Netherlands, which control the emergency supplies that would replace Soviet gas, could come under intense pressure to refuse emergency sharing. Norway, a possible reserve source in the 1990s, could be particularly vulnerable to Soviet pressure, given its common border with the USSR and its disputes with the Soviets over Svalbard and offshore energy resources.[32] Strong domestic criticism of NATO in either of these countries (e.g., in the Norwegian Labor Party) could also undermine European solidarity.

Finally, a Soviet energy embargo directed at Western Europe would be unlikely to enhance solidarity in the Atlantic Alliance. Events since the 1979 Soviet invasion of Afghanistan have shown that East-West crises exacerbate rather than narrow the differences between the United States and Western Europe. A severe energy crisis in Europe could intensify what one observer has called "the politics of resentment" against the United States.[33] Difficulties in Europe—financial, economic, or political—quickly engender charges on both the left and the right that the United States is "exploiting" Europe's misfortunes to reexert dominance over the old continent.

---

[32]The Soviets might, for example, stage large naval maneuvers in the vicinity of Norwegian offshore oil-production facilities. Some experts doubt that Norway will ever have much surge capacity in a crisis, "since the transmission system from the offshore fields will need to run very close to capacity to keep the export projects commercially viable." (Stern, *International Gas Trade in Europe*, p. 161).

[33]Josef Joffe, "Europe and America: The Politics of Resentment (Cont'd)," *Foreign Affairs*, Vol. 61, No. 3 (1983).

In what was a fairly characteristic remark at the time, French Socialist party leader Mitterrand charged during the 1973–1974 oil embargo that "the U.S. profits from the situation in order to reinforce their economic domination over Western Europe."[34] In France, this sentiment was shared by Socialists, Gaullists, and Communists, and in Britain, by elements on the right of the Conservative party. The British and French governments refused to support joint action with the United States against the Arabs and called instead for a special Euro-Arab dialogue. The Heath and Pompidou governments proposed a triangular arrangement in which Arab oil producers would channel their excess revenues to Egypt, which would then agree to buy industrial products in Europe. Such purchases would enable the West Europeans to afford the higher prices for OPEC oil. While Britain returned to a more Atlanticist policy under a new Labour government, France went ahead with its bilateral approach, concluding agreements with the principal Middle Eastern oil-producing states on the exchange of French goods for guaranteed supplies of oil.

Although the United States probably would not make a large contribution to relieving shortages resulting from a gas embargo (although under IEA arrangements, it is committed to sharing supplies in an oil shortage), solidarity between it and Western Europe would be important for political and psychological reasons. Greater hardship in Europe than in the United States would not be conducive to maintaining this solidarity, however. It is not overly harsh to remark that the European countries are "free riders" to one degree or another. At best, they might be willing to sacrifice if their main ally was sacrificing at least as much and probably a good deal more than they were. If this were not the case, as it probably would not be in an energy crisis, the mood in Europe could quickly degenerate into one of self-pity and resentment directed at the United States as much as at the Soviet Union. American efforts to prevent the West Europeans from seeking a "compromise" on Soviet terms would lack credibility, much the way British exhortations to the French in 1940 to continue fighting against the Germans were often greeted with cynicism. Soviet propaganda would no doubt seek to foster the idea that European leaders were "pawns" of the United States and that Europe was being made to suffer for American interests. These charges would find a receptive audience among significant minorities in all the West European countries and would complicate government efforts to maintain resistance in the face of Soviet pressure.

---

[34]Quoted in Lieber, *Oil and the Middle East War*, p. 27.

Supply Cutoff: Conclusions

For the remainder of this decade, the Soviet Union is unlikely to try to exert leverage on Western Europe by threatening a gas embargo. Its share of West European energy supplies will be too low and the world energy market too glutted to make such a threat credible. If for some reason the Soviet Union were to order an embargo, there is a good chance that the USSR would be the net loser and the United States would be a beneficiary. An abortive cutoff would lead to a loss of Soviet hard-currency earnings, loss of the Soviet Union's reputation as a reliable supplier, and perhaps a tougher West European policy toward the East. In the 1990s and beyond, the Soviet Union could be in a stronger position to exercise leverage, and the West European countries will have to undertake measures in the next few years to head off the development of a new vulnerability.

The least predictable aspect of Western Europe's potential vulnerability to an actual or threatened supply cutoff is the political aspect. West European officials confidently claim that if the Soviet Union were to interrupt supplies, the West European countries, having made substantial investments in diversification and other emergency measures, could rebuff any attempt at leverage. Such confidence may or may not be warranted, but it is impossible to prove the case one way or the other. A Soviet gas cutoff probably would occur only in a severe East-West crisis, and there is reason to question whether governments would be as decisive under these circumstances as they now claim they would be. It is important to stress, however, that a breakdown of West European resolve in a crisis would occur not in response to economic factors, but largely because of political and military pressures that fall outside the bounds of economic leverage. Whether economic leverage would add in a significant way to political and military leverage is difficult to judge.

On the one hand, it can be argued that Soviet leverage over Western Europe is basically political and military—or even purely military—and that economic pressure contributes little to advancing Soviet influence on the continent. On the other hand, it is possible to argue that Soviet leverage is the result of an accumulation of factors—military, political, economic, propaganda, and so forth—and that the pipeline contributes, if only in a small way, to the Soviet Union's overall ability to influence West European behavior. Although considerable evidence suggests that the Soviets themselves take the view that influence results from an accumulation of many factors, West European governments for the most part do not share that view. They appear to believe that the Soviet Union confronts the Atlantic Alliance with an essentially political and military threat. According to this view, if in a severe crisis the Alliance succeeds in countering this threat, the added effects of economic leverage, to the extent that they operate at all, will not tip the balance in the direction of Western collapse. If, on the other hand, the Alliance cannot stand up to Soviet political and military pressure, invulnerability to economic leverage will be of no avail in any case.

LONG-TERM DEPENDENCE

The supply-cutoff scenarios discussed above are all based on the assumption that either Western Europe or the Soviet Union precipitates a radical shift in current policy, perhaps in the wake of developments in volatile third areas such as Eastern Europe or the Middle East. This section discusses a less dramatic scenario, the emergence in one or more major European countries of a politically significant economic dependence on the Soviet Union.

This possibility has received considerable attention in recent months in various U.S. and U.S.-West European forums. Slow economic growth, high unemployment, and a perception of Europe's lagging performance in high-technology areas have led some American observers to suggest that Western Europe might be forced to turn increasingly to the Soviet Union as a market and that ever-increasing levels of trade will lead to Soviet leverage over Europe.[35] The pipeline, which was the largest East-West deal ever and was clearly motivated by concern about jobs in declining industries, has become a symbol of the potential complementarity between Western Europe and the East.

Although Western leaders generally dismiss claims that economic complementarity leads to political accommodation, even conservatives and members of the business elite recognize a degree of "objective convergence" between Soviet interests and their own. According to Fiat chairman Giovanni Agnelli, for example, "Europe's and Japan's need for primary commodities and energy resources, together with the Soviet Union's need for manufactures and advanced technology, creates condi-

---

[35]Former Chancellor Helmut Schmidt took cognizance of (and rejected) this possibility at the Georgetown CSIS conference in Brussels on The Future of NATO and Global Security (H. Peter Dreyer, "Europeans Discuss Economic Issues," *Journal of Commerce,* January 17, 1984). The popular literature on Europe's "decline" has burgeoned on both sides of the Atlantic. See, for example, "Executives Assess Europe's Technology Decline," *The Wall Street Journal,* special supplement, February 1, 1984; Lawrence Minard, "Can Europe Catch Up?" *Forbes,* July 4, 1983; "The Decline of Europe," *Newsweek,* April 9, 1984; and the cover story, "Deutsche Industrie: verschlafen wir die Zukunft?" *Der Spiegel,* No. 52, 1983.

tions of 'complementarity' among these economies which do not exist to the same degree between the American and Soviet economies."[36]

The extent to which this complementarity gives the Soviet Union political leverage over West European policy is difficult to determine and is judged differently by different observers. It could be argued that all substantial trading relationships (including the American grain trade with the Soviet Union) result in some degree of leverage, because trading partners are somewhat more reluctant than they might be in the absence of trade to endanger their economic interests by precipitate political moves, and because various domestic interest groups become dependent on maintenance of the trading relationship. In the case of Western Europe, however, it is difficult to tell whether trade with the Soviet Union creates any *additional* reluctance on the part of West European governments to incur Soviet displeasure beyond that which arises from the politically motivated West European interest in détente. In any case, by agreeing to deploy new American missiles in the face of Soviet protests and despite Soviets hints that trade might suffer, the major West European countries have shown an ability to defy the Soviets on important issues.

Soviet spokesmen claim that there is an emerging complementarity between Eastern and Western Europe and have hailed it as a positive step. They attribute to it, in part, West European reluctance to follow the U.S. lead on policy toward the Eastern bloc, especially where trade and technology transfer are concerned. Vadim Zagladin, the First Deputy Head of the International Department of the Central Committee, wrote in a French newspaper that in his view, "the formation of a system of complementarity among national economies" was taking place in Europe.[37]

Most West European business and political leaders do not agree with Zagladin that the level of trade with the Soviet Union is high enough to give either side politically useful leverage. The literature on economic warfare and leverage tends to support this view. Compared with past situations in which trade led to political influence, Western Europe's level of trade with the Eastern bloc is quite low. In his classic study of Nazi Germany's economic penetration of the Balkans, Albert O. Hirschman calculated that in 1938 Germany accounted for 52 and 59 percent, respectively, of Bulgarian imports and exports. Levels of German trade were also high in other countries of the region, all of

---

[36]Giovanni Agnelli, "East-West Trade: A European View," *Foreign Affairs,* Vol. 58, No. 5 (1980), p. 1021.

[37]*Le Matin,* July 13, 1981.

which were smaller and less developed than Hitler's Germany.[38] In contemporary Western Europe, not even Finland begins to approach such levels of trade with the Soviet Union. In West Germany, the NATO country with the greatest stake in East-West trade, exports to the Soviet Union peaked in 1975 at 3.1 percent of total exports, then declined to a low of 1.9 percent in 1981 before rising again to 2.2 percent in 1982 and 2.5 percent in 1983.[39] Sales to Eastern Europe as a whole accounted for 5.7 percent of German exports in 1983.

Those who argue that the Soviet Union does exercise political influence over Western Europe through trade tend to dismiss these aggregate figures; instead, they point to concentrations in particular industrial sectors, the power of certain interest groups, and other factors that in their view magnify the political importance of East-West trade. The following discussion examines both sides of this question, considering the economic and political factors in Western Europe that could lead to increased Soviet leverage. It focuses in particular on the contribution the energy trade might make to such leverage.

Economic Factors

As the controversy over the pipeline recedes, it becomes increasingly clear that the attraction of the project was not the gas alone but the promise of jobs and export orders that it entailed.[40] In addition to the substantial contracts for the project itself, the pipeline would assure a steady flow of hard currency to the USSR, enabling the Soviets to continue to buy European goods. Unlike the Reagan Administration, West European governments do not believe that limiting Soviet access to hard currency is desirable. Indeed, West German officials go so far as to suggest that the pipeline was necessary in order to channel hard currency to the Soviet Union and thus enable it to maintain trade with the West. According to West German Foreign Minister Genscher,

---

[38]*National Power and the Structure of Foreign Trade,* Publications of the Bureau of Business and Economic Research, University of California Press, Berkeley, 1945.

[39]Data for 1983 are from Lothar Julitz, "1984 wird ein gutes Exportjahr," *Frankfurter Allgemeine Zeitung,* March 29, 1984; data for earlier years are from U.S. Department of State, Bureau of Intelligence and Research, *Trade of NATO Countries with European CEMA Countries, 1979-1982,* November 28, 1983.

[40]David Brand, "Europeans Subsidized Soviet Pipeline Work Mainly to Save Jobs," *The Wall Street Journal,* November 2, 1982; and Axel Lebahn, "The Yamal Gas Pipeline from the USSR to Western Europe in the East-West Conflict," *Aussenpolitik,* Vol. 34, No. 3 (1983).

if Europe were to go back on [the pipeline] deal . . . it would mean a drastic reduction in trade throughout the entire decade of the 1980s. The foreign currency earnings resulting from the additional Soviet gas exports to Western Europe made possible by the construction of the Yamal Pipeline are not likely to offset even the loss of income resulting from the expected decrease in Soviet oil exports to Western Europe. If the Soviet Union is denied these earnings, this would be bound to lead to a sharp decline in trade because of the Soviet lack of foreign currency.[41]

The concern expressed by Genscher about the health of the Soviet market inevitably raises questions about how dependent the FRG and other West European countries are on this market. As noted above, the Soviet share of the West German market is not comparable to the shares achieved by countries that have in the past used trade as an instrument of political control. Nonetheless, the Soviet Union is the largest West German market outside the OECD. It ranks above Saudi Arabia, Iran, Iraq, Nigeria, and Brazil, and is thus the largest West German market for goods appropriate for industrializing countries. The United States is a larger market, but it buys a different mix of products from the FRG than do the CMEA countries (e.g., a high proportion of automobiles). West Germany depends on other West European countries for 68 percent of its exports, but of the remaining 32 percent, the Soviet Union accounts for a substantial 8.5 percent, and the Communist bloc as a whole accounts for nearly 17 percent.[42]

In certain sectors, the Soviet Union's share of German exports is larger than its share of total trade. In the export-dependent machine-tool industry, the USSR takes 11 percent of German exports;[43] for many machine-tool firms, the Eastern bloc takes as much as 50 percent.[44] In the metals sector, Mannesmann, a participant in the Urengoi project, sells 50 percent of its large-diameter pipe to the Soviet Union—9 million tons in the last decade.[45] In the late 1970s, CMEA countries accounted for 25 percent of German export orders for turnkey industrial plants. This figure dropped to 10 percent in the early 1980s as these countries ran into debt problems, but it is expected to rise again in coming years.[46]

---

[41]Genscher, "Toward an Overall Western Strategy for Peace, Freedom and Progress," p. 55.

[42]Jess Lukomski, "Bonn Seeking Closer Moscow Trade Ties," *Journal of Commerce,* November 15, 1983.

[43]Ibid.

[44]Wolfgang Hoffmann, "Fuer den Osten nichts Neues," *Die Zeit,* May 13, 1983.

[45]"Ramponierte Bereiche," *Der Spiegel,* No. 8, 1984.

[46]Jonathan Carr, "Orders for Plant Stabilising," *Financial Times,* March 22, 1984.

Although West German exports to the East comprise a relatively limited share of total exports and an even more limited share of total GNP, their importance to a few major industries assures a powerful political constituency for East-West trade. Genscher's Free Democratic Party, which controls both the Foreign Ministry and the Economics Ministry, is the most pro-business party in Germany and a powerful advocate of expanding East-West trade. All the parties favor increased trade with the East, however, with the Social Democratic Party (SPD) motivated as much by political as economic concerns, and the Christian Democrats mainly motivated by the interests of West German business. The largest German trade union, the metalworkers union, exerts pressure on all the parties, but especially the SPD, for increased trade with the East. The banks are also a powerful lobby in favor of trade. They have lent enormous sums to the East that could be put at risk if the bloc were deprived, as was Poland, of means to earn hard currency. Indeed, because the banks would also suffer if the large steel and machinery companies that depend on the Eastern market should collapse, they are doubly vulnerable to any cutback in trade ties.

To assess whether economic ties will increase to the point that they lead to greater Soviet influence over Western Europe, it is necessary to look at trends in Western Europe's trade with the East. On the export side, government and industry officials in Europe generally reject the view that West European industry is "structurally dependent" on the East. However, many of these officials are concerned about certain imbalances in the European economies that could lead to a relative increase in the importance of the Soviet market. With the economic recovery that began in 1983, these concerns have abated somewhat, although not entirely.[47]

In 1984, the five leading economic research institutes in West Germany published their second "structural report" on the state of the German economy.[48] The report attempted to shed light on West Germany's relative position in the world economy, particularly on its competitive performance over the past decade. It examined relative performances in exporting high-growth *products* (e.g., office equipment and microprocessors) and in exporting to high-growth *markets* around the world.

---

[47]Siemens officials claim that the technological gap between Germany on the one hand and the United States and Japan on the other has been exaggerated and will be closed by the end of the decade ("Siemens To Increase Product Technology," *Financial Times,* April 12, 1984).

[48]Sigrid Matern-Rehm, "Missed the Train After All?" *Wirtschaftswoche,* January 27, 1984, in JPRS, *West Europe Report,* March 20, 1984.

On the product side, the institutes found that there was "a heavier concentration on groups [of products] with a stagnating or declining share in world trade" in Germany than in the United States or Japan. On the market side, the institutes did not find that West Germany (or the EC as a whole) became increasingly dependent on the Eastern market in the 1970s. Indeed, West German exports to the Centrally Planned Economies (CPEs) as a percentage of total exports actually registered a small decline over this period. However, the institutes did conclude that West Germany performed poorly in growth markets. As Table 2 shows, the explosion in exports to the OPEC countries (from 3.3 to 8.3 percent of total exports) masked a stagnant or declining share of trade with other growth areas.

Table 2

EXPORT PERFORMANCES ON THE WORLD MARKET
(Percent of total exports)

	Exporter									
	World		FRG		EC		U.S.		Japan	
Market	1972	1981	1972	1981	1972	1981	1972	1981	1972	1981
FRG	10.1	8.7	—	—	13.2	11.0	5.5	4.4	3.2	3.9
France	6.7	6.6	12.7	12.9	9.8	9.7	3.6	3.3	0.9	1.5
UK	7.0	6.3	4.8	6.8	5.2	6.8	5.3	6.1	3.4	3.2
Italy	4.4	4.3	8.0	8.1	5.8	5.9	2.5	1.9	0.8	0.6
Belgium	4.2	3.7	7.8	6.9	6.7	6.1	2.3	2.6	1.2	1.0
Netherlands	4.9	4.3	10.2	8.4	7.3	6.2	2.7	3.4	1.5	1.3
Total EEC	39.2	35.8	45.8	45.4	50.4	48.4	22.6	22.5	11.4	11.9
U.S.	15.6	14.3	9.6	6.8	8.5	6.3	—	—	31.3	25.6
Japan	3.0	4.0	1.4	1.2	1.1	1.1	7.5	7.0	—	—
Other industrial	18.8	15.3	28.1	26.0	23.0	20.2	36.7	27.4	12.4	10.2
Total industrial	76.6	69.4	79.8	74.3	78.3	71.5	66.1	56.4	54.2	46.7
Asian NICs[a]	3.3	5.2	1.0	1.4	1.1	1.6	3.9	6.3	11.5	12.9
Latin NICs[a]	2.4	2.7	2.3	2.0	1.7	1.6	7.8	11.0	2.4	2.5
OPEC	3.7	8.6	3.3	8.3	3.9	10.1	5.9	10.4	6.6	15.2
Other LDCs	10.8	10.9	8.5	9.3	11.1	11.9	15.6	14.2	20.2	16.5
Total LDCs	20.3	27.4	15.0	21.0	17.9	25.1	33.1	41.8	40.7	47.2
CPEs	3.1	3.2	5.2	4.6	3.8	3.4	0.8	1.8	5.1	6.1
World	100	100	100	100	100	100	100	100	100	100

SOURCE: The second "structural report" on the state of the German economy, published by the five leading West German economic research institutes, 1984.
[a]Newly industrialized countries.

The institutes concluded that the developments analyzed "should be an occasion for profound thought. If West Germany's enterprises cannot gain a stronger foothold on the world's dynamic markets, then the basis for the German real wage level, which is relatively high when compared to international levels, will be in danger. Increasing sales on already established and stagnating markets would probably be possible only through price cuts."[49] In many ways, this warning about the future could apply retrospectively to the pipeline project, where manufacturers sold equipment at loss-making prices in order to maintain production and, in the case of AEG-Kanis in Germany and John Brown in Britain, to stave off bankruptcy. The very fact that such warnings are being made in Europe, however, should help to mitigate concerns in the United States about the prospects of an increasing West European dependence on the Soviet market. West European businessmen, economists, and government officials are aware that turning to the Soviet Union would not be a solution to Western Europe's economic difficulties, but in fact would become an economic problem in its own right that would lead to lower profits, wages, and living standards—in addition to the political difficulties associated with such a move. They will therefore need relatively little encouragement from the United States to undertake measures to strengthen West European economies in ways that will have the effect (if not the intent) of lowering dependence on markets in the East.

A struggle clearly is under way in and among the EC countries to determine whether the Community develops further into a protectionist system of industrial and agricultural subsidies, or whether it will dismantle some of its protectionist practices and move toward more open trading arrangements and integration in world markets. It is likely that neither pure protectionism nor free trade will prevail completely, and that the EC will remain a semi-protectionist (with state subsidies considered a protectionist mechanism) bloc with a selective commitment to free trade. Whatever path the EC development follows, however, Community political and business leaders, while likely to remain unresponsive to U.S. efforts to further limit trade, technology, and credit flows to the Soviet Union, will see little advantage in far-reaching integration of their economies with the CMEA countries. The EC states are determined to participate in the world economy across a full range of high technology, basic industrial, and agricultural

---

[49]Ibid. It should be pointed out that the implications of declining industrial competitiveness are particularly serious for Germany in view of the large percentage of German workers still employed in manufacturing: In 1982, 43.5 percent of German workers were employed in industry, compared to 30.1 percent in the United States, 35.2 percent in France, and 35.3 percent in Japan (*OECD Observer*, No. 121, March 1983).

products, and they appear willing to take action to carve out (or in some cases retain) positions in these markets. Many of these actions will involve state subsidies and covert and overt protectionism and will therefore lead to continued *commercial* tensions between the EC and all its major trading partners—the United States, Canada, Australia, New Zealand, Japan, the newly industrialized countries (NICs), and the poorer developing countries. However, with regard to *security,* these actions will at least have the effect of limiting the degree of EC trade dependence on the Eastern market.

In addition to trends on the export side, i.e., the competitive standing of West European industry in third markets, the future of Western Europe's economic relations with the Soviet Union will be determined by the amount of hard currency the Soviet Union has available to import products from Western Europe. The latter will in turn depend on the performance of the Soviet Union's own energy export sector, on price trends in world oil and natural-gas markets, and on the amount of hard currency the Soviets will be required to expend for competing products (notably grain).

The prevailing view among experts is that the Soviet Union's exportable energy surplus will not expand dramatically and will thereby set an upper limit on both Western Europe's energy dependence and the level of Soviet industrial purchases in the West.[50] This view is based on three assumptions: (1) that Soviet oil production will level off and decline; (2) that domestic consumption requirements will remain high; and (3) that large exports to Eastern Europe will continue to preempt Soviet sales to the West.

Although in the long run these assumptions are likely to prove valid, for the last several years all three have been wrong. In what was clearly a high-priority program aimed at maintaining hard-currency earnings, in the early 1980s the Soviets took a number of steps that enabled them not simply to maintain but actually to increase their oil exports to Western Europe. Oil sales to Western Europe reached a record 1,320,000 barrels per day in 1982, up from slightly over 1 million barrels in 1981.[51] Together with new and existing gas sales, these levels of oil exports enabled the Soviets to strengthen their hard-currency reserves and to pay for imports.

A number of factors helped the Soviets to achieve these objectives. Until as recently as October 1983, Soviet production of oil continued to increase, albeit slowly. On the demand side, the Soviets had some

---

[50]"Soviet Oil Export Drop Held Limiting Trade," *Journal Of Commerce,* September 21, 1983.

[51]CIA, *International Energy Statistical Review,* various dates.

success in their domestic conservation efforts, which were helped along by relatively slow (by Soviet standards) economic growth. Eastern Europe was forced to cut back its imports of Soviet oil through conservation and by finding alternative suppliers. Soviet exports of oil to Eastern Europe peaked at around 1.6 million barrels per day in 1980 and 1981, and then dropped to a little over 1.4 million barrels per day in 1982.[52]

The Soviets are likely to rely on this same combination of measures for the remainder of the decade to maintain their hard-currency earnings.[53] But even with such efforts, a large upsurge in hard-currency earnings and, by extension, import capacity from the West is probably out of the question. Since the October 1983 peak, there has been a modest decline in oil production in the Soviet Union. Some experts believe that the late 1983–1984 trend marks the long-awaited beginning of a substantial decline in production. Others think it is too early to draw such a conclusion and point out that such a decline, even if it does occur, is likely to be gradual and will commence from a very high level of production.[54] Whatever the truth regarding trends in the Soviet oil industry, a large increase in production is extremely unlikely. The Soviets also will be unable to further cut back their exports to Eastern Europe. The 200,000-barrel-per-day reduction early in the decade was a one-time adjustment that will not be repeated. Similarly, cutting domestic consumption of oil in the Soviet Union holds some promise, but it is likely to be a slow process that will yield results only gradually.

Over the long term, the outlook for the Soviet energy sector and the USSR's hard-currency earning situation could improve. The Soviet Union is engaged in major infrastructural projects in all branches of energy production and transport that should in time strengthen its position in world hard-currency energy markets. It still generates a high proportion of its electricity with petroleum, and the completion of an ambitious (but troubled) nuclear power program will free up oil for

---

[52]Ibid. Nikolai Baibakov, the head of Soviet Gosplan, stated, "In the forthcoming years we will increase production, but the rate of growth will be significantly lower than hitherto and will demand serious expenditures . . . I have to say that it would not be realistic to expect us to increase our oil deliveries." (Budapest Television Service, April 1, 1984, in Foreign Broadcast Information Service, *Daily Report: Soviet Union*, April 4, 1984).

[53]See Jan Vanous, "The Impact of the Oil Price Decline on the Soviet Union and Eastern Europe," *The Energy Journal*, Vol. 4, No. 3 (1983), p. 14.

[54]"No Cause for Concern on Soviet Oil Output," *East-West*, March 13, 1984. There has been recent high-level concern in the Soviet Union about the performance of the oil-extraction sector (Serge Schmemann, "Pravda Assails Oil Industry for Lag in Siberian Output," *The New York Times*, April 4, 1984).

export. The CMEA states have also agreed to construct another natural-gas pipeline to Eastern Europe that will allow a gradual cutback in Soviet oil exports to Eastern Europe and their replacement with gas. This too will free up more oil for export to the West.

The Soviets have proposed the construction of additional pipelines to Finland and the linkup of the Soviet and Norwegian gas networks. They also reached agreement with Turkey in October 1984 on construction of a pipeline that by the end of 1986 will permit exports of up to 6 billion cubic meters of gas annually,[55] and they obtained Turkish agreement for the construction of a second line for the import of Soviet-generated electricity.[56] Even the troubled coal industry has begun to export, supplying not only Eastern Europe, but also Greece, Turkey, some Middle East countries, and Scandinavia.[57] To permit the export of Siberian coal, the Soviet Union is also expanding port facilities in the Far East.[58] It remains to be seen, of course, whether all these ambitious investments will be completed and whether markets for all Soviet energy products will be found. There can be little doubt, however, of the Soviet Union's intent to become an increasingly important force in world energy markets.

In the tightened energy markets that are expected after 1990, the Soviet Union could tempt the West Europeans to increase their purchases of Soviet energy, particularly if such purchases can be tied to a new round of industrial exports. The past has also shown that rapid changes in energy prices, such as may well occur in the late 1980s or early 1990s, can create a momentum in the direction of higher trade. Since both sides prefer balanced trade and neither wants the level of its exports reduced, there is a tendency, following a change in prices that leaves one side or another in temporary deficit, to reestablish the balance by leveling up the export volume of the country in deficit rather leveling down its import volume.

---

[55]Albert Axebank, "Turkey To Be Big Buyer of Soviet Natural Gas," *Journal of Commerce,* October 11, 1984. Western observers report that the Soviet Union moved quickly in 1982 to undercut efforts by Iran to strike a gas deal with Turkey by offering to build a pipeline and supply gas at low prices. By doing so, the Soviets not only secured the Turkish market for themselves, but they removed Turkey's incentive to participate in any effort to link Iran directly to Western Europe by a pipeline through Turkey. After the Soviet Union, Iran has the world's largest reserves of natural gas, and it is in the Soviet commercial and political interest to eliminate potential markets for Iran's gas—other than the one in the south of the USSR. See Stern, *International Gas Trade in Europe,* p. 48; and Youssef M. Ibrahim, "Iran To Supply Natural Gas to Turkey," *The Wall Street Journal,* September 13, 1982.

[56]David Barchard, "Moscow To Send More Energy to Turkey," *Financial Times,* January 30, 1984.

[57]Art Garcia, "Slump in Coal Exports Nears End, but New Markets Doubtful Till '90," *Journal of Commerce,* November 14, 1983.

[58]Albert Axebank, "Expansion Under Way at Port in Soviet Union," *Journal of Commerce,* November 14, 1983.

The point is illustrated by Finland's experience. As long as demand for energy remained high in Finland and world energy prices were at record levels, the Finns steadily increased their exports to the Soviet Union without unbalancing the bilateral clearing arrangement that regulates Soviet-Finnish trade. When Finland's demand for energy declined and world prices dropped, however, the Finns were left with a huge export surplus that the Soviets were not prepared to tolerate. Soviet trade officials began to exert pressure on the Finns to purchase more manufactured products.[59] Failing to find acceptable products, the Finns had little choice but to increase their purchases of energy from the Soviet Union.[60] Although until the late 1970s Finland had pursued a policy of not allowing dependence on Soviet energy to rise above 20 percent of total imports, by 1983 this level had reached 90 percent.[61] This increase in the level of dependence came about not as a result of the need for Soviet energy as such—the period was one of worldwide energy glut—but because ever-higher levels of energy imports were accepted as payment for industrial goods.

What occurred in Finland has only partial relevance for the rest of Western Europe. One factor that distinguishes the major West European countries from Finland is sheer size. The Soviet Union is able to provide 90 percent of Finland's energy imports and purchase 27 percent of its total exports. It would not be possible for it to achieve a similar degree of penetration—even if that were politically possible—in countries whose economies range from 7 (Italy) to 14 (West Germany) times the size of Finland's.

Nonetheless, there are parallels. Large Soviet exports of natural gas under long-term contract have raised the prospect of sustained deficits in Western Europe's trade with the Soviet Union. To correct this imbalance, West European governments are pressing the Soviets to buy more from their manufacturers. If energy prices continue to fall as they have through the 1980s, the West Europeans may go too far in their efforts to balance trade with the Soviet Union and may accumulate trade surpluses that the Soviets will be reluctant to accept. Governments might be left, as were the Finns, with a choice between accepting still greater amounts of Soviet energy (assuming the non-availability of other products) and cutting back their exports. As the

---

[59]"More Emphasis on Compensation Purchases from USSR," *Helsingin Sanomat*, August 17, 1983, JPRS *West Europe Report*, September 13, 1983.

[60]Albert Axebank, "Finns Work To Maintain Brisk Soviet Trade," *Journal of Commerce*, March 29, 1984.

[61]"Finland Buys Soviet Oil To Maintain Trade Balance," *Journal of Commerce*, September 20, 1983.

Finnish experience suggests, slashing the level of exports is politically the more difficult course of action.

In the case of both rising and falling world energy prices, there is a danger that the interaction between energy imports and industrial exports may exert upward pressure on the volume of trade. This interaction is reinforced by the fact that so much of what West European firms have to export and what the Soviets are eager to import contributes, over the long term, to the Soviet ability to produce, distribute, and export energy. Despite efforts by the West Europeans to sell to the food, automotive, and other sectors of the Soviet economy, energy remains the priority sector for trade. The French have been awarded a contract for $380 million to develop a gas complex in Astrakhan.[62] French companies are also engaged in discussions about exporting civilian nuclear technology to the Soviet Union.[63] The West German government is wary of a second pipeline project but is backing West German participation in other energy projects. Mannesmann, for example, is discussing possibilities for creating a coal gasification industry for the Soviets.[64] Norway is hoping to supply offshore oil technology to the Soviets that would help them develop the Barents Sea.

European (and to some extent U.S.) efforts to assist the Soviets in developing their energy sector could enable the USSR to increase its exports in the 1990s. If the prices at which these increased exports are traded rise at some point (many forecasters foresee sharp rises in the world price of energy in the early 1990s), the problem of a trade surplus on the Soviet side will return, bringing yet another cycle of West European development projects in the Soviet Union and higher levels of trade.[65]

Political Factors

Although in theory the West European states are committed to an open, liberal economic order (some, such as West Germany and the Netherlands, more than others), all are in varying degrees attracted to what might be called "mercantilist-statist" rather than "liberal" approaches to economic interdependence. All associate export success

---

[62]"East-West Traders Raise the Curtain," *Economist,* January 7, 1984.

[63]"Why Paris Is Peddling Its Nuclear Wares in Moscow," *Business Week,* December 26, 1983.

[64]John Tagliabue, "Mannesmann in Talks on Soviet Coal Project," *The New York Times,* May 27, 1983.

[65]It should be pointed out that Western efforts to develop the Soviet energy sector will have the beneficial effect of helping to moderate increases in the prices of oil and gas on world markets.

with special trading relationships based on cultural-historical ties and military and/or political influence. Despite their rhetorical commitment to economic liberalism, West European leaders seem to look to high-level political arrangements as at least a partial solution to the challenge of international economic competition. The perennial hope is that special political arrangements will guarantee a market for European products, even if these products are higher-priced or less technologically advanced than those offered by competitors. At various times, European hopes have been fixed on Africa, with its colonial past; on the Arab world, with its proximity to Europe and its hostility to U.S.-supported Israel; on Latin America, with its special "Latin" affinity to France and its reservations about U.S. dominance; and, political and military circumstances notwithstanding, Eastern Europe, with its historical and cultural ties to the rest of Europe.[66]

As hopes for economically advantageous special relationships with various international blocs or groupings have all been disappointed to one degree or another, the CMEA countries have taken on greater significance as Western Europe's special area of "influence." Some businessmen believe that the Eastern bloc and especially the Soviet Union offer the last—indeed, the only—remaining possibility for Western Europe to establish the kind of special relationship that will help to sell its goods. Interest in such complementary economic ties is reinforced by pessimism about Western Europe's long-term economic prospects and its ability to compete successfully with Japan, the NICs, and the United States.[67]

A comprehensive relationship with the East is appealing throughout Western Europe, particularly in West Germany. Although West Germany's economic and political ambitions were directed westward after World War II, a remnant of the former interest in *Mitteleuropa* survives.[68] Eastern Europe is for Germany what Africa is for France and the Commonwealth is for Britain: a special zone that acts toward it with a deference that derives from (and perhaps serves to compen-

---

[66]There are also industry-specific variants. For example, in its campaign to create a major electronics industry, the current French government is counting on forming alliances with important third world countries such as India and Brazil which share (the French hope) a desire to cut back the power of American companies such as IBM (John Elliott, "France Set To Aid Indian Electronics Industry," *Financial Times*, December 16, 1983).

[67]For a good example of this "Europessimism," see Wolfgang Hager, "Protectionism and Autonomy: How To Preserve Free Trade in Europe," *International Affairs*, London, Vol. 58, No. 3 (1982).

[68]The Soviet Union is not part of *Mitteleuropa*. However, the West Germans, because of their experiences in the 1960s with the policy of "small steps" toward Eastern Europe and its ultimate collapse with the 1968 Soviet invasion of Czechoslovakia, do not believe that it is possible to deal with these countries without "going through Moscow."

sate for the loss of) former great-power status. Trade with the East is also an important element in the West German policy of attempting to diminish the effects of the division of Europe and holding open the possibility of some form of reunification of the German nation.

If the search for special political relationships is the positive element in European mercantilism, the negative element is a deep-seated suspicion of the United States as a commercial competitor. In France especially, there is a tendency to regard American economic liberalism as an ideology that serves the interests of the militarily and economically strongest power, and one that justifies efforts on the part of France to use its political influence to advance its own economic interests. To one degree or another, this feeling is generalized throughout Western Europe.

Business and government elites in the West European states often suspect that the United States uses its political, military, and economic power to deprive them of influence around the world. This feeling developed after World War II, when the United States pressed for the dismantling of the British, French, and Dutch empires and of the British system of imperial preference. It did so, many in Europe suspected, for its own commercial gain.[69] Along with trade and monetary affairs, energy is an area in which European resentment of the United States and the feeling that the United States uses its size and political leverage to compete unfairly with Western Europe have been particularly strong. West Europeans, particularly the French and the British, resented the U.S. use of its political power to (in their view) help American oil companies displace their European competitors from the Middle East, especially Saudi Arabia.[70] In the late 1950s, it was Enrico Mattei's resentment of the oil majors that led Italy to make common cause with the Soviet Union in an effort to break the power of the "seven sisters."[71]

This deep suspicion of American commercial motives dies hard in Western Europe and was, as a West German banker intimately involved in the pipeline negotiations has noted, a definite factor in

---

[69]Richard Gardner, *Sterling-Dollar Diplomacy*, Oxford University Press, New York, 1956.

[70]See the excellent case study by Robert O. Keohane, "Hegemonic Leadership and U.S. Foreign Economic Policy in the 'Long Decade' of the 1950s," in William P. Avery and David P. Rapkin (eds.), *America in a Changing World Political Economy*, Longman, New York, 1982. Keohane cites the conclusion of the Church subcommittee report on multinational corporations that "the French never forgave the Americans for keeping them out of Saudi Arabia" (p. 73). Keohane argues that it was the Saudis who wanted the French kept out of Saudi Arabia.

[71]P. H. Frankel, *Mattei: Oil and Power Politics*, Praeger, New York, 1966.

Europe's rush to build the pipeline.[72] In the early 1970s, the swiftness with which American business was moving into major projects like the Kama River truck plant and the since canceled "North Star" project, in conjunction with the U.S.-Soviet political détente, raised fears that the United States might deprive the West Europeans of economic influence in this region, much as it had in the Middle East and in the former colonies of the European states:

> This U.S. commitment [to the Kama River plant] demonstrated to Western Europeans that the Americans could soon outpace them in business with the Soviet Union once they deliberately set about bidding for contracts on a massive scale. Nothing may have come of wishful thinking about U.S.-Soviet cooperation, but the shock U.S. competition created at the time still wields its deep-seated implicit effect on many Western European businessmen. It has found expression in Western Europe's political disputes with the U.S.A. in the twofold suspicion that America begrudges Europe the erstwhile North Star (now Yamal) project and is determined to torpedo the Yamal project and interrupt economic ties between the Soviet Union and Western Europe on a lasting, long-term basis in order, by concentrated deployment of U.S. capital and technology, to be even more matchless in exploiting Siberian natural resources. So the Yamal project bore the seeds of political mistrust and fear of competition among Western partners before it even saw the light of day as far as the public was concerned.[73]

The belief that American policy on East-West trade is motivated less by genuine concern about security than by commercial interests and a desire to prevent Europe from competing in high-technology industries is never far from the surface in Western Europe. (These suspicions, it must be stressed, have been fed by inconsistencies in U.S. policy over the years and above all by the policy of continuing grain sales while seeking curbs on the export of other goods.)[74] Although originally strongest in conservative and business circles, suspicion of U.S. motives has been taken up by the left and by anti-American circles in most of the countries of Western Europe.

In an article devoted to the troubles of the West German machinery industry, the German weekly *Der Spiegel* asserted that "the United States government would love to stop business deals by German plant builders with the East bloc entirely. While President Ronald Reagan makes sure that his farmers can sell their wheat to the Soviet Union,

---

[72]Lebahn, "The Yamal Gas Pipeline from the USSR to Western Europe in the East-West Conflict," op. cit.

[73]Ibid., pp. 264–265.

[74]Of course, when the United States *did* institute a grain embargo, European officials were no more willing than previously to cut back industrial trade with the Soviet Union. See Otto Wolf von Amerongen, "Economic Sanctions as a Foreign Policy Tool?" *International Security*, Vol. 5, No. 2 (1980), pp. 159–167.

the eastern trade of the Europeans bothers him." The analysis concludes: "The intention is recognizable; an important competitor of
American concerns would be hard hit [by a cutoff of trade with the
East]—last year German firms delivered plants worth DM 2.7 billion to
Eastern European countries."[75] Similar complaints were heard in 1984
in Britain when an internal memorandum was leaked from ICL, the
leading British computer company, charging that U.S. controls on
exports of high technology to the East, ostensibly designed to stop strategic equipment from reaching the USSR, were actually intended to
strengthen the U.S. technological lead over European competitors.[76]
Along these same lines, the West German Institute for the Study of the
German Economy (DIW) issued a report charging that "the motive of
U.S. high technology protectionism does not lie in the security field, as
is often claimed. The real aim is to protect the domestic high technology industry, which saw its traditional lead endangered in the light of
Japanese successes."[77] The French newspaper *Le Monde,* irritated at
U.S. opposition to French plans to sell telephone exchanges to the
Soviet Union and Bulgaria, charged that "taking advantage of its political, technological, and military power, and of the anxieties engendered
by Moscow's policy, the United States intends to increase its tutelage
over its partners.... Deprived of outlets to the third world because of
insolvency, and to the Eastern bloc countries because of embargoes,
and urged to open their markets to U.S. firms, leading European and
also Japanese industries are highly likely to encounter difficulties. And
this will benefit their competitors on the other side of the Atlantic."[78]
The attributing of U.S. policy on trade to a desire to "hit" competitors
was carried even further by the left-wing daily *Frankfurter Rundschau,*
which not only claimed that U.S. efforts to block the pipeline could
"easily be explained as a policy to promote exports of the United
States' own coal and gas," but attributed U.S. opposition to high-
technology sales to the East to an "intention to exclude the East bloc
as a possible competitor on the world market for high quality finished
goods."[79]

These charges are of course absurd—no one is more opposed to the
Reagan Administration's export control policies than the U.S. business
community, the alleged beneficiary of these policies. Their very

[75]"Maschinenbau: ganz duester," *Der Spiegel,* No. 45, 1983.

[76]Christian Tyler, "U.S. Regulations Stifle Computer Trade, Says ICL," *Financial Times,* February 17, 1984.

[77]Jonathan Carr, "Institute Accuses U.S. of 'High-Tech Protectionism,'" *Financial Times,* August 16, 1984.

[78]Editorial, *Le Monde,* August 11, 1984.

[79]Editorial, *Frankfurter Rundschau,* November 18, 1982.

absurdity, however, points up the deep strain of self-pity and suspicion of U.S. motives that exists in Europe and that is by no means confined to the left of the political spectrum. This suspicion facilitates de facto alliances between the business- and elite-centered right-wing anti-Americanism in Europe and the left-wing anti-Americanism centered in political, journalistic, and academic circles.

Counterbalancing these negative attitudes toward the United States as a commercial competitor is a continued West European interest in economic ties with American firms. With the rise of the dollar and the accelerated growth in the U.S. economy, the West European countries have begun to register large surpluses in their trade with the United States and have made major gains in third markets at the expense of U.S. exporters. In some cases, notably Pan Am's huge order for European Airbuses, U.S. customers have played a major role in determining the fortunes of European high-technology industry.

A few signs indicate that some European officials and businessmen appreciate the "locomotive" role of the U.S. economy since 1982. On balance, however, praise for U.S. efforts is rare in European settings and is overshadowed by continual complaints about U.S. budget deficits, technology transfer policies, and (impending) protectionist legislation. As U.S. economic growth slows and European trade surpluses with the United States diminish, European complaints if anything will grow more insistent. Continued West European resentment of the U.S. economic role in the world may not in itself drive Western Europe into increased dependence on the Soviet Union. It will, however, make it increasingly difficult for West European governments to discuss East-West trade in an atmosphere that it not at least somewhat poisoned by anti-Americanism.[80]

The Middle East Connection

Perhaps the greatest imponderable in this discussion of structural change in Western Europe and vulnerability to Soviet leverage concerns the Soviet role in the Middle East. The most serious threat that the Soviet Union could pose to Western Europe's energy security is of course a thrust toward the Persian Gulf that would result in Soviet control of a large share of Western Europe's oil supplies. As noted

---

[80]A growing school of left-wing economists in Western Europe argues that the United States deliberately fosters tensions with the Soviet Union in order to exert economic leverage over Europe. See Christian Deubner, "Change and Internationalization in Industry: Toward a Sectoral Interpretation of West German Politics," *International Organization*, Vol. 38, No. 3 (1984); and Ekkehart Krippendorff and Michael Lucas, "One Day We Americans Will Have To Consider the Destruction of Europe," in Rudolf Steinke and Michael Vale (eds.), *Germany Debates Defense*, M. E. Sharpe, Armonk, New York, 1983.

earlier, this analysis of the pipeline's potential as an instrument of leverage assumes that no seizure of the Gulf takes place. Such a development would render the pipeline virtually irrelevant in a conflict that could lead (under the Carter Doctrine) to military conflict between the Soviet Union and the United States. However, it is necessary to examine whether, short of a direct Soviet seizure of the Gulf, Soviet political and economic influence in the Middle East could combine with Soviet control over a portion of Western Europe's natural-gas supplies to yield an unacceptable degree of leverage.

Europeans themselves frequently cite a connection between Soviet-West European and Soviet-Middle Eastern relations when they argue that cooperation in the development of Soviet energy resources will help to prevent a Soviet thrust toward the Middle East. It has also been noted that the Soviets, particularly during the oil shocks of the 1980s, sought to promote a set of triangular political and economic relationships among the Soviet Union, Europe, and the Middle East. In early 1980, shortly after the Soviet invasion of Afghanistan and at the height of the post-Shah oil crisis, Soviet spokesmen put out feelers about prospects for using CSCE as an umbrella organization for a system of three-way guarantees among Western Europe, the Soviet Union, and the Middle Eastern oil producers. These proposals were aimed at blunting U.S. efforts to mobilize its allies in response to the invasion of Afghanistan, even as they subtly underlined for the West Europeans the Soviet Union's own growing interest in the Persian Gulf region and its potential influence there.[81]

Despite talk by both the West Europeans and the Soviets about linkages between developments in the three regions, Soviet-West European, Soviet-Middle Eastern, and West European-Middle Eastern relations remain for the most part a series of parallel relationships, with relatively few triangular interactions. Contrary to West European claims, there is no reason to believe that the Soviet Union has been deterred from seeking to increase its influence in the Middle East by enhanced energy cooperation with the West. Indeed, by trying to convince Iran and the Arab states that it is the energy-short West rather than the Soviet Union that has designs on the Gulf, the Soviets seek to use their energy abundance as a propaganda asset in their efforts to expand their influence in the region.

---

[81]According to Moscow TASS (February 29, 1980): "It is quite feasible to include problems of the security of oil communications and equal commercial access to oil sources of the Persian Gulf region in the agenda of the all-European conference on energy, which has been proposed by the Soviet Union. All countries which have signed the Helsinki Final Act could jointly submit to the United Nations proposals concerning appropriate guarantees which would be accepted by this world forum. If the Eastern countries which possess oil agree to this, the United Nations could extend such guarantees to cover the territorial integrity and independence of these countries."

If Western Europe's economic and political ties with the Soviet Union do little to discourage and perhaps even create added incentives for Soviet activism in the Middle East, it is also correct to say that Soviet efforts to induce Western Europe and the Middle East into a set of triangular economic, political, and security arrangements have met with little success. The diplomatic proposals of 1980 received almost no support in either Europe or the Middle East. The USSR has been somewhat more successful on the purely commercial level, establishing itself as a factor in the Middle Eastern energy trade. As will be seen, however, this success rests to a great extent on special and in many cases temporary factors.

In 1982, the Soviet Union imported an average of 197,000 barrels of Middle Eastern oil per day—with the exception of the embargo year of 1973, the highest total ever—equivalent to 6 percent of total Soviet exports or 13 percent of exports to the non-Communist world.[82] By 1983, the Soviet Union was importing 250,000 barrels of Middle Eastern oil per day. Experts believe that in 1984, Soviet purchases of Middle Eastern oil will average 300,000 barrels per day. The Soviet Union is also trying to develop its gas links with the Middle East. Until trade was stopped by the Khomeini regime, Soviet gas imports from Iran averaged over 9 billion cubic meters per year, an amount that until 1976 was greater than total Soviet gas exports to Western Europe.[83] Because there is no alternative market for this gas, the Soviets paid low prices for it to Iran, while selling their own gas to Western Europe at world levels. The Soviet Union also imports some 2.4 billion cubic meters of gas per year from Afghanistan.[84] In a pattern that was established even before the 1979 invasion, Afghan gas is sold to the Soviet Union at very low prices (again because of the absence of an alternative market) in exchange for goods rather than hard currency.

Not surprisingly, the Soviet Union is trying to increase the scope of this triangular trade, which eliminates the need for transportation over long distances inside the USSR and thus lowers costs to the Soviet economy. In addition, the price differential between the imported and exported gas results in a substantial profit. The prospect of barter payments to Middle Eastern states, assured since 1979 in the case of Afghanistan and possible in the case of a new agreement with Iran, further increases the advantages for the Soviet Union in that it assures

---

[82]CIA, *International Energy Statistical Review,* various dates.

[83]CIA, *International Energy Statistical Review,* December 20, 1983, p. 24.

[84]This figure is calculated from one given by Kabul Radio and reported in Amity Shlaes, "Afghan Resources Flowing to U.S.S.R. Despite the War," *The Wall Street Journal,* January 17, 1984. It is broadly in line with CIA figures in *International Energy Statistical Review,* December 20, 1983.

a substantial gain in hard currency. Although relations between the USSR and Iran remain very poor, the Soviets have displayed interest in resuming the natural-gas trade with Iran.[85] Despite the fighting in Afghanistan, the Soviet Union has continued to develop an infrastructure within the country that will enable increased extraction and export of gas to the captive Soviet market.[86]

Whether the Soviet Union increases its role as a middleman in the energy trade or whether this role remains limited is a key question that will affect the future of Soviet relations with Western Europe. Absent a Soviet military thrust toward the Persian Gulf, it seems that the second alternative is more likely. The Soviet Union is able to obtain the oil it imports or retrades from the Middle East mainly because Iran, Iraq, and Libya, all of whom import Soviet weapons, use barter with the Soviet Union to circumvent OPEC production quotas.[87] If world oil markets were to tighten, these countries presumably could sell the same oil for hard currency and probably would sever their connection with the Soviet Union. The sale of gas by Afghanistan and (formerly) Iran to the Soviet Union resulted from special circumstances that are unlikely to arise in other countries. But Soviet activities in the region do indicate a continuing interest in establishing triangular political, economic, and security relationships with Europe and the Middle East and serve as a reminder that Western Europe's energy security is very much tied to developments in the Middle East. Any improvement in Soviet prospects in the region could multiply the leverage potential of the gas pipeline and could require a reevaluation of Western Europe's vulnerability to Soviet leverage.

Long-Term Dependence: Conclusions

Although there is some danger that Western Europe's economic problems could lead to dramatically increased levels of trade with the Soviet Union and that increased trade in turn could create political leverage, on balance, this possibility must be judged unlikely. Trade is starting from relatively modest levels, and prospects for further expansion will be limited by a number of factors. Most European businessmen and government officials do not regard the Eastern market as a solution to their economic problems and are concentrating on

---

[85]Albert Axebank, "Soviets Say Iran Lost $5 Billion in Gas Shutoff," *Journal of Commerce,* November 4, 1983.

[86]Michail Nazarow, "Moskaus langfristige Plaene in Afghanistan," *Neue Zuercher Zeitung,* January 29, 1983.

[87]Data based on Wharton Econometrics analysis, reported by Amity Shlaes, "Soviets Help OPEC Members Undercut Minimum Price," *The Wall Street Journal,* January 27, 1984.

developing new markets and new products that may actually lower the importance of sales to the East. In any case, the Soviet Union will have difficulty earning the hard currency to pay for increased imports.

This is not to say that Western Europe and the United States will cease to clash over East-West trade. In numerous instances European governments will look to the Soviet Union to help troubled companies in troubled sectors of the economy.[88] With high unemployment in Western Europe persisting despite the resumption of economic growth, saving jobs will remain a political priority. The Belgian government's defense of a sale of a Belgian-made machine tool believed destined for a Soviet missile plant on the grounds that the manufacturer was near bankruptcy illustrates the kinds of problems that will arise.[89] Moreover, Western Europe's move into high technology, although it may in the long run prevent the emergence of dependence on the Soviet market, will itself create pressures to sell to the East. Already, European companies worried about breaking into the market for advanced telephone exchanges are lobbying their governments for permission to sell to Bulgaria, the Soviet Union, and Hungary. Nor is it correct to conclude that the days of massive credit-financed projects in basic industries are over. As a prominent U.S. economist has observed, "One of these days a Soviet delegation is going to show up in Duesseldorf and announce that they would like to rebuild their railroad system. And then over sherry they might just drop that they expect the Germans to finance several billion dollars worth of steel, locomotives, and other exports. And what do you think the Germans will say?"[90]

For many reasons, then, friction between the United States and Western Europe over trade with the East will continue. The West Europeans will remain committed to this trade and will see it as at least a partial solution to problems in basic and high-technology industries. From the U.S. perspective, however, the main significance of this trade will be the effect it has on strengthening the military and industrial capacity of the Soviet Union, either by transferring high technology or, perhaps more important, by applying European industrial and financial power to the solution of sectoral problems in the Soviet economy (gas distribution, nuclear power, rail transportation), rather than the effect it has in strengthening Soviet influence over particular West European political decisions.

---

[88]Much the way that the United States is counting on increased sales to the Soviet Union to mitigate the severe problems in the U.S. agricultural sector.

[89]See "Get Rich Quick" (editorial), *The Wall Street Journal*, August 21, 1984.

[90]Remarks by Gregory Grossman, European-American Institute Workshop, Ditchley, England, May 18–20, 1984.

IV. CONCLUSIONS

This report has considered Western Europe's vulnerability to two scenarios in which the Urengoi-Uzhgorod pipeline could play a role. The first involves a sudden cutoff of gas supplies aimed at extracting political concessions. The second involves an economically induced realignment of Western Europe away from the Atlantic Alliance and toward the Soviet Union. Both scenarios are possible, but neither could be categorized as probable. As bad or worst-case possibilities, however, they merit serious attention.

It is not difficult to puncture many of the arguments West European governments have put forth to support the claim that the pipeline could not be used as an instrument of political pressure. The Soviet Union has not been a reliable supplier in situations where it has had the upper hand, and Soviet and Arab "reliability" really cannot be compared, since the USSR and the Arab world stand in very different positions relative to Europe. Arguments about diversity and flexibility of supply are likewise problematic, since even a minor shortage of gas could be harmful if prices shot up dramatically, if the cutoff were seen as a prelude to military attack, or if European countries could not agree on common measures to replace embargoed supplies. Puncturing these arguments does not, of course, *prove* that the Soviet Union would interrupt supplies in a crisis, nor does it guarantee that in the event the Soviet Union did order an embargo, it would be able to obtain major political concessions from the West European states. Indeed, an ill-conceived gas cutoff would have enormous economic and political costs and could benefit the United States rather than the Soviet Union.

Similarly, it is possible to construct a scenario in which the pipeline helps encourage economic developments in Western Europe that lead to increased Soviet influence over security and defense matters. Western Europe could turn increasingly to the East to market its industrial products. In payment for these products, it would import ever larger amounts of energy. This in turn would undermine efforts to develop Europe's own resources and diversify sources of supply. It would also undermine the purchasing power of OPEC and African states and would thus make Europe even more dependent on the East as an export market. The entire scenario would be further complicated if the Soviet Union were to increase its influence in the Middle East and become an arbiter between it and Western Europe.

Here again, outlining such a possibility does not make it a probability. For such a scenario to be plausible, current trends must be extrapolated over many years, perhaps an unlikely prospect. Leaving aside any political resistance to such a development in Europe, the Soviet Union will not have the import or the export capacity to achieve a degree of economic dominance over its trading partners comparable to that exercised by countries that have used trade as an instrument for political leverage in the past. Economic dependence on the Soviet Union would be partial and probably would be only a contributing factor in an overall setting of Soviet dominance, the major underpinnings of which would be political and military.

If neither of these scenarios—cutoff or structural dependence—is likely in its worst-case form, the mere fact that both are even possible offers some insight into Europe's current situation. Europe is vulnerable. The fact that the pipeline was built at all was an admission on the part of governments of an existing vulnerability. Western Europe needed the gas and it needed the jobs. The relevant issue is therefore not vulnerability as such, but the way in which the pipeline increased or in some way changed Western Europe's already vulnerable position in the post-oil-crisis world. This vulnerability is likely to remain a factor in U.S.-West European relations, no matter how East-West trade in energy develops.

BIBLIOGRAPHY

Allen, Robert Loring, "Economic Warfare," *International Encyclopedia of the Social Sciences,* Vol. 4., 1968.

——, *Soviet Economic Warfare,* Public Affairs Press, Washington, D.C., 1960.

Bailey, Richard, "Impact of the Euro-Soviet Gas Pipeline," *National Westminster Bank Quarterly Review,* August 1982.

Boyes, Roger, "Siberian Gas for Europe," *Europe,* No. 225, May-June 1981.

CIA, *International Energy Statistical Review,* various dates.

Commission of the European Communities, *Communication from the Commission to the Council Concerning Natural Gas,* Brussels, April 9, 1984.

Crovitz, Gordon, "The Soviet Gas Pipeline: A Bad Idea Made Worse," *The World Economy,* Vol. 5, No. 4 (1982).

Frankel, P.H., *Mattei: Oil and Power Politics,* Praeger, New York, 1966.

Gustafson, Thane, *The Soviet Gas Campaign,* The Rand Corporation, R-3036-AF, Santa Monica, California, June 1983.

Hirschman, Albert O., *National Power and the Structure of Foreign Trade,* Publications of the Bureau of Business and Economic Research, University of California Press, Berkeley, 1945.

Klinghoffer, Arthur Jay, *The Soviet Union and International Oil Politics,* Columbia University Press, New York, 1977.

Lebahn, Axel, "The Yamal Gas Pipeline from the USSR to Western Europe in the East-West Conflict," *Aussenpolitik,* Vol. 34, No. 3 (1983).

Matthies, Klaus, "Soviet Natural Gas—A Threat to Western Europe's Security?" *Intereconomics,* September/October 1981.

Maull, Hans, "Das Erdgas-Roehrengeschaeft mit der Sowjetunion: Gefahr fuer die wirtschaftliche Sicherheit?" *Europa Archiv,* No. 24, 1981.

Pakravan, Karim, *Oil Supply Disruptions in the 1980s,* Hoover Institution Press, Stanford, California, 1984.

Rahmer, B.A., "Soviet Union: Big Gas Deal with West Europe," *Petroleum Economist,* Vol. 49, No. 1 (1982).

Russell, Jeremy, "Import of Soviet Gas by Western Europe," *NATO's Fifteen Nations,* December 1982/January 1983.

Stent, Angela, *Soviet Energy and Western Europe,* Washington Papers, No. 90, 1982.

Stern, Jonathan P., *International Gas Trade in Europe: The Policies of Exporting and Importing Countries,* Heinemann Educational Books, London, 1984.

U.S. Department of State, Bureau of Intelligence and Research, *Trade of NATO Countries with European CEMA Countries, 1979–1982,* November 28, 1983.

Vanous, Jan, "The Impact of the Oil Price Decline on the Soviet Union and Eastern Europe," *The Energy Journal,* Vol. 4, No. 3 (1983).

Wiles, P. J., *Communist International Economics,* Basil Blackwell, Oxford, 1968.